"This book has be⬚⬚⬚⬚ ⬚⬚⬚ ⬚⬚⬚⬚ paring me for my ⬚⬚⬚ ⬚⬚⬚⬚⬚⬚ ⬚⬚⬚ ⬚⬚⬚⬚ tured activities and assuring gui⬚⬚⬚⬚⬚ ⬚⬚⬚⬚⬚ throughout has helped me identify the mechanisms that will enable me to be at my best during part-time study. I now feel prepared, excited and confident about my next steps."

Jo Goodman, *PhD Student, Lancaster University*

"This book is grounded in real world experiences. Offering activities that help readers to apply the guidance it offers, and with a living archive of blogs to accompany it, *Thriving in Part-Time Doctoral Study* will be invaluable to anyone even thinking about doing a part-time doctorate."

Kelly Louise Preece, *University of Exeter*

Thriving in Part-Time Doctoral Study

Thriving in Part-Time Doctoral Study is a practical guide, designed to support part-time doctoral researchers in navigating their learning experience and providing them with the tools they need to succeed in academia, alongside the work and life challenges they may be facing. Featuring eight highly practical chapters, this book covers every aspect of the part-time doctoral journey from initial planning right through to completion.

Easy to dip in and out of with realistic advice, learning points and reflective activities based on real experiences, this book:

- Reflects a diversity of voices across academic disciplines
- Features real-world examples from doctoral researchers
- Can be referred to throughout the doctoral journey

This key resource will support the reader in considering how best to access and draw on the communities of support available, get the most from a supervisory team, and build professional networks. It recognises that each student's learning pathway is different and offers support to allow each individual to take control and make it *their* part-time doctorate.

Jon Rainford is a Staff Tutor in Education, Childhood, Youth and Sport at The Open University, UK. He is also a Visiting Research Fellow in Education at The University of Bath, UK.

Kay Guccione is Head of Research Culture and Researcher Development at the University of Glasgow, UK. She is a National Teaching Fellow, specialising in doctoral supervision, mentoring and community building for researchers.

Insider Guides to Success in Academia

Series Editors:
Helen Kara,
Independent Researcher, UK and
Pat Thomson,
The University of Nottingham, UK.

The *Insiders' Guides to Success in Academia* address topics too small for a full-length book on their own, but too big to cover in a single chapter or article. These topics have often been the stuff of discussions on social media, or of questions in our workshops. We designed this series to answer these questions in to provide practical support for doctoral and early career researchers. It is geared to concerns that many people experience. Readers will find these books to be companions who provide advice and help to make sense of everyday life in the contemporary university.

We have therefore:

(1) invited scholars with deep and specific expertise to write. Our writers use their research and professional experience to provide well-grounded strategies to particular situations.
(2) asked writers to collaborate. Most of the books are produced by writers who live in different countries, or work in different disciplines, or both. While it is difficult for any book to cover all the diverse contexts in which potential readers live and work, the different perspectives and contexts of writers goes some way to address this problem.

We understand that the use of the term 'academia' might be read as meaning the university, but we take a broader view.

Pat does indeed work in a university, but spent a long time working outside of one. Helen is an independent researcher and sometimes works with universities. Both of us understand academic – or scholarly – work as now being conducted in a range of sites, from museums and the public sector to industry research and development laboratories. Academic work is also often undertaken by networks that bring together scholars in various locations. All of our writers understand that this is the case, and use the term 'academic' in this wider sense.

These books are pocket sized so that they can be carried around and visited again and again. Most of the books have a mix of examples, stories and exercises as well as explanation and advice. They are written in a collegial tone, and from a position of care as well as knowledge.

Together with our writers, we hope that each book in the series can make a positive contribution to the work and life of readers, so that you too can become insiders in scholarship.

Helen Kara, PhD FAcSS,
independent researcher
https://helenkara.com/
@DrHelenKara (Twitter/Insta)
Pat Thomson PhD PSM FAcSS FRSA
Professor of Education, The University of Nottingham
https://patthomson.net
@ThomsonPat

Books in the Series:

Planning and Passing your PhD Defence
A Global Toolbox for Success
Olga Degtyareva and Eva O.L. Lantsoght

Refining Your Academic Writing
Strategies for Reading, Revising and Rewriting
Pat Thomson

Thriving in Part-Time Doctoral Study

Integrating Work, Life and Research

Jon Rainford and Kay Guccione

Routledge
Taylor & Francis Group

LONDON AND NEW YORK

Designed cover image: © Getty Images

First published 2024
by Routledge
4 Park Square, Milton Park, Abingdon, Oxon OX14 4RN

and by Routledge
605 Third Avenue, New York, NY 10158

Routledge is an imprint of the Taylor & Francis Group, an informa business

© 2024 Jon Rainford and Kay Guccione

The right of Jon Rainford and Kay Guccione to be identified as authors of this work has been asserted in accordance with sections 77 and 78 of the Copyright, Designs and Patents Act 1988.

All rights reserved. No part of this book may be reprinted or reproduced or utilised in any form or by any electronic, mechanical, or other means, now known or hereafter invented, including photocopying and recording, or in any information storage or retrieval system, without permission in writing from the publishers.

Trademark notice: Product or corporate names may be trademarks or registered trademarks, and are used only for identification and explanation without intent to infringe.

British Library Cataloguing-in-Publication Data
A catalogue record for this book is available from the British Library

Library of Congress Cataloging-in-Publication Data
Names: Rainford, Jon, 1982- author. | Guccione, Kay, author.
Title: Thriving in part-time doctoral study: integrating work, life and
research / Jon Rainford and Kay Guccione.
Description: New York : Routledge, 2023. | Series: Insider guides to
success in academia | Includes bibliographical references and index. |
Identifiers: LCCN 2022060332 (print) | LCCN 2022060333 (ebook) | ISBN
9781032109657 (hbk) | ISBN 9781032122885 (pbk) | ISBN 9781003223931 (ebk)
Subjects: LCSH: Universities and colleges--United States--Graduate work. |
Part-time college students--United States. | Study skills.
Classification: LCC LA228.5 .R3 2023 (print) | LCC LA228.5 (ebook) | DDC
378.1/550973--dc23/eng/20230308
LC record available at https://lccn.loc.gov/2022060332
LC ebook record available at https://lccn.loc.gov/2022060333

ISBN: 978-1-032-10965-7 (hbk)
ISBN: 978-1-032-12288-5 (pbk)
ISBN: 978-1-003-22393-1 (ebk)

DOI: 10.4324/9781003223931

Typeset in Helvetica
by SPi Technologies India Pvt Ltd (Straive)

Contents

Figures

Introduction

Using this book

Who is this book for and how should I use it?

This book has been primarily written for those of you who have already started on a part-time doctorate or who are about to embark on this exciting next step in your career. It can be worked through in a logical manner or can be used to dip in and out of when you face specific challenges or situations. Much like the doctorate itself, which is an iterative process, this book is likely to be something you come back to at relevant times throughout your doctorate. You might also find it a valuable tool in deciding if a part-time doctorate is right for you and if so, what form it should take. It is also likely to be invaluable for people supporting doctoral researchers in either a formal or more informal manner. Therefore, this book can be used independently by doctoral researchers or collaboratively with peers or supervisors to think about or discuss the issues the book raises.

Being able to share our thoughts with you is a real privilege and we hope that they give you a basis to consider how these ideas might impact upon your doctorate. Think of it like a travel guide for your doctorate. Your journey may not be in the order that we have presented the ideas

DOI : 10.4324/9781003223931-1

and that is OK. Feel free to jump to the sections that are relevant for you at any given time. It is important to note that whilst your focus is often on the thesis itself (after all, we have all been daunted by the "thing" we have to produce) this book is about far more than the thesis. We want to help you develop your mindset and identity as a researcher.

As this book is part of the *Insider Guides to Success in Academia* series, this volume takes a handbook format; it is a practical guide that offers you realistic advice based on real experiences. We have purposefully avoided densely referenced text that can be distracting, and instead we offer you a conversational tone throughout. We want to speak to you like we would to the colleagues we work with and support.

Why can our experience help you navigate your doctorate?

Jon completed his part-time PhD in Education at Staffordshire University in 2019. He juggled working on his thesis with working in higher education for five years. During this time, he experienced changes to his supervisory team, went through a redundancy, and changed jobs twice more. He also had to contend with personal issues, including losing his dad just after his graduation after a three-year battle with lung cancer. As such his experience was not always smooth. The concept for this book came from Jon's wish he had had a similar reference when he embarked upon his PhD.

Kay did not do her PhD part time, and, being in a scientific discipline, did not work alongside many others who were studying part time. Following her PhD and postdoctoral research, Kay moved into a career path as a researcher development professional and has now worked for many years to design the educational frameworks and support structures that help researchers through their doctorates and forwards within their choice of career path. Early on in her developer career, it became clear to Kay that researchers who studied part time had different concerns about their doctorate, and different learning pathways through the process. Part-time researchers were generally more skilled and experienced in the workplace and brought many valuable assets to their departments of study. They also tended to be more pressed for time, and experienced tighter constraints on how they used this time and how they partitioned study in their life. In recognition of the vast diversity of the people who engage in part-time research degrees, Kay sought specifically to bring together part-time researchers, and learned a great deal from these communities. She is exceptionally grateful for their input into her learning.

We, Kay and Jon, both bring unique understandings of the part-time journey, and have consciously used our different perspectives to ask ourselves questions about how a part-time experience can be seen as a distinct and positive approach. Using our coaching skills honed as facilitators, tutors, and mentors, we developed a series of discussions and engaged part-time researchers with them. We also put these questions out more widely, to people in our expanded disciplinary and professional networks, to make sure that we drew upon a breadth of different experiences and opinions in presenting our advice and points for reflection. Whilst we have led on different parts of this book, it is the product of two unique perspectives and co-authored throughout.

Is this book for me?

There are a whole host of different doctoral journeys and whilst books often focus on full-time study, a large proportion of these journeys are part time. It is also not uncommon for people to switch modes during their doctorate (Gardner and Gopaul, 2012). Chapter 1 will give you a glimpse at just how diverse these are. Beyond the type of doctorate, your own life situation makes your doctoral journey unique. This might be down to geography, stage of life, caring responsibilities, employment context, disability, or many other factors. As such we have tried to incorporate a wide range of voices and experiences within this volume. Each chapter includes *real-world reflections* based on either single students or constructed from a number of actual students' experiences. We hope these will help bring some richer context to the chapters. We conclude each chapter with a *researcher's recommend* section to offer some practical takeaways you can use to help you on your journey.

We have deliberately chosen not to apply our own interpretations to the *real-world reflections*. Whilst some have been edited for brevity, these are the voices of people like you who are doing or have done a part-time doctorate. Some may resonate and others might not. Take some time to think about them and how they may or may not mirror your own experiences. Although we wish we could have included many more experiences, we have tried to offer a range of insights that address some of the issues you might be trying to make sense of on your own journey.

Whilst this book aims to cover a wide range of issues and challenges relating to the part-time doctoral journey, like any guidebook, there are only so many landmarks we can include. To help this be as valuable as possible for your own journeys, we have incorporated several elements in each chapter to help you personalise your experience and get the most out of this book. Each chapter features activities to help you reflect upon how the ideas we present may help you during your doctorate. This book also dovetails into others in the *Insider Guides to Success in Academia* series, which are signposted in relevant sections of the book. These are also likely to help with the practicalities of studying at a distance (McChesney et al., forthcoming), writing your thesis (Thomson, 2023), or planning your route to publication (Salmons and Kara, 2020).

Different experiences, similar challenges

We have written this book in a UK context but have focused on issues that are likely to resonate on a wider scale. Whilst there may be significant local differences in the format and structure of doctorates, especially professional doctorates (Jones, 2018), many of the concerns transcend national borders. For example, Bates and Goff (2012), who undertook part-time doctorates in Canada, highlighted that flexibility was a key reason for undertaking their part-time doctorates, as was often the case for those we talked to during the process of writing this book. They also reflected upon the interrelation between paid work and the doctorates, and especially the impact this had upon time management. These are issues that recur in the stories throughout this book. The unpredictability of life challenges that impacted progress also resonate with the *real-world reflections* in this book. In the Australian context, Mantai (2019) highlights that exclusion and isolation can be key issues for part-time doctoral researchers trying to be part of a research culture. Their research also highlighted gaps between what institutions offer and what students need – again, an issue that seems to span continents. We therefore hope that this book helps signpost support outside of your institutions and provides the mechanism to fill some of these gaps.

Where will this book take you?

The eight chapters of this book cover all the key aspects of the doctorate. You may come to this before you begin your doctorate, in which case start at the beginning and work through. However, if you are well on your journey you might want to focus on a specific topic. We offer a brief outline of each chapter here to help you work out what is relevant.

Starting at the beginning, **Chapter 1** sets the scene for the doctorate. You may be about to start, or may be some way into the process, but were you aware of the vast array of doctorate types there are? This chapter will help you understand the differences. This chapter is also about identifying what you want from your doctorate. If Chapter 1 is about the what, **Chapter 2** focuses on the why, upon identifying your personal goals, what you need to know to succeed in the doctorate, and planning out your journey. Even if you started some time ago, the information and activities can be a useful way to regroup and reconnect with the reasons you chose this journey.

Developing your identity as doctoral researchers is the focus of **Chapter 3**. For many of you this will likely involve juggling both professional and student identities. For others though, it might just be about helping understand how the "you" that is doing your doctorate fits in with your other personal identities. This chapter offers several practical activities and case studies to help you think about these key issues. This is complemented by **Chapter 4**, which helps you consider the professional relationship with your supervisor. It also offers supervisors an insight into some of the distinct skills part-time researchers might bring to a doctorate and how these might be accompanied by specific challenges. It is likely to be useful to work through this together to help develop an effective relationship, and this chapter offers two specific activities to help with this.

Chapter 5 moves the focus onto practical issues surrounding managing the doctorate. Building on the planning started in Chapter 2, this chapter explores the practicalities of managing the doctorate as a project. For many readers, this may be the largest project you have managed, so this chapter offers practical tips and tools to support you. Other readers may find here a different perspective to previous experiences of managing projects, or suggestions for how to adapt their professional experience to the doctorate. Alongside managing the project, managing yourself is important. **Chapter 6** argues why it is important for you to maintain balance and breaks to successfully complete the doctorate. There are some real-world reflections and activities to help you think about this and plan for keeping that balance.

It can be common to think of the doctorate as a solo endeavour, but **Chapter 7** looks at the importance of support for thriving during your doctorate. In this chapter we help you think through ways to connect with other people and the existing connections you might have, or new connections you may wish to forge both online and offline. These connections can be vital for success but harder to develop and maintain compared to full-time colleagues, so this chapter offers some practical suggestions to help.

In **Chapter 8**, the book concludes by tackling the issue of what's next and how you might build on the skills, experiences, and knowledge you gain during the doctorate. It can be tempting just to focus on the thesis as the end goal but in this chapter we help you to consider your next steps as you reach the end of this significant milestone.

About the activities

The range of routes through the part-time doctorate are very diverse. Added to this, your individual experiences and circumstances will be necessarily unique, and so we have offered you 19 opportunities to stop and reflect on how our guidance matches your own needs and preferences. These are presented as learning activities and are placed at important points throughout this book. Stopping to reflect on what you have read – and how this applies to you specifically – will greatly increase the usefulness of this book. To get the maximum value from these pieces of personal reflection, it would be helpful to visit them in order. However, as with the whole book, you can dip in and out of the activities that interest you, or that offer value to you at a particular time.

If the language and activities we have used do not appeal to you or resonate, feel free to answer the question in the way that works best for you. If you don't know how to answer a question or haven't thought about it before, it is OK to come back to it later. Feel free to also be as creative as you like, you might like to represent your thoughts visually or as voice notes. If you do something really creative, share it with us on social media using #ThrivingPartTime.

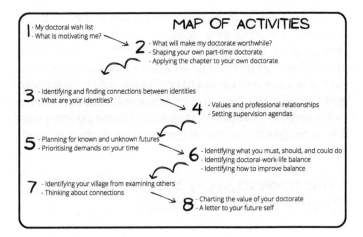

Figure 0.1 Activity map

One book, many possible routes

Trying to capture every part-time experience in a book of this size would be impossible. We have aimed to include a breadth of voices and experiences from individuals on a range of different types of doctorates and working across different disciplines. That said, we cannot capture everything within these covers and we see this book as part of a wider set of resources we have curated for you.

Alongside writing this book we have been curating advice, tips, and stories from current and previous part-time doctoral students at www.thrivingparttime.com. This living archive supplements the book and will hopefully provide a source of inspiration, or particular case studies related to your own doctoral journeys. We also hope you will consider sharing your own stories and advice there to help future readers of this book, especially if you do not see yourself represented in what we have written or featured.

One way we have found of taking these conversations forwards and gathering opinions on specific topics is through a live synchronous chat on Twitter, also known as a tweet chat. You can find an archive of these conversations on the website and we would encourage you to think about hosting one if you have a topic you want to discuss that is not covered in this book. We have also included guidance on the webpage on how to manage one of these chats yourself.

This book has only been possible thanks to our own village

We would not have the richness of detail within this book without the numerous conversations both of us have had online and offline with so many different researchers, supervisors, and researcher developers. In particular, we would like to thank every single person who has contributed to the blog and to our tweet chats, as well as the authors of the *real-world reflections* in the book: Nicole Brown, Karen Campbell, Julia Everitt, Selina Griffin, Louise Harris, Sharon Inglis, Mel Simms, Dawn Weeden, and those who wished to remain anonymous.

We would also like to thank our beta readers who offered their thoughts on early drafts of some chapters: Beverley Jennings, Sally Sharp, Jackie King-Owen, Kim Collett, Matt Offord, Jo Sutherst, Martin Wain, and Sue Williams. Additionally, we would like to thank the four anonymous beta reviewers that provided comments on the draft of this book. Their engagement and feedback have helped strengthen it further. Of course, in our village we also include the series editors Helen Kara and Pat Thomson, who have supported this project from its inception along with Sarah Hyde, Molly Selby, and Zoe

Thomson at Routledge. We'd also love you to become part of our village by adding your voice to this conversation.

References

Bates, P. and Goff, L. (2012) 'The invisible student: Benefits and challenges of part-time doctoral studies', *Alberta Journal of Educational Research*, 58(3), 368–380.

Gardner, S. K., & Gopaul, B. (2012) 'The part-time doctoral student experience', *International Journal of Doctoral Studies*, 7, 63–78. doi:10.28945/1561

Jones, M. (2018) 'Contemporary trends in professional doctorates', *Studies in Higher Education*, 43(5), 814–825. doi: 10.1080/03075079.2018.1438095

Mantai, L. (2019) '"A source of sanity": The role of social support for doctoral candidates' belonging and becoming', *International Journal of Doctoral Studies*, 14, 367–382. doi: 10.28945/4275

McChesney, K., Burford, J., Frick, L. and Khoo, T. (forthcoming) *Doing Doctoral Research by Distance: Navigating Off-campus, Online, Hybrid, and Cross-national Doctoral Study*. Abingdon: Routledge.

Salmons, J., and Kara, H. (2020) *Publishing from Your Doctoral Research. Create and Use a Publication Strategy*. Abingdon: Routledge.

Thomson, P. (2023) *Refining Your Academic Writing: Strategies for Reading, Revising and Rewriting*. Abingdon: Routledge.

1 What is a part-time doctorate?

By the end of this chapter you will

- Have a better understanding of the range of different routes a part-time doctoral researcher can follow.
- Understand the benefits of a part-time doctorate and how it can enrich you and your research.
- Be able to identify what has brought you to the part-time doctorate and what will sustain you through the doctoral journey.

What's in store

The doctorate takes diverse forms, and in modern times has adapted to accommodate and encourage participation by different types of learners from different educational backgrounds and career contexts. In this chapter we draw upon the decision-making narratives of two part-time researchers, who share with us how they made their choice to pursue a particular mode of study. We hope you will find these informative as you consider your own doctorate wish list. Two introductory guided activities will support you to consider your options for your doctorate, and

DOI : 10.4324/9781003223931-2

to ask yourself the big question every researcher should know the answer to – "why am I doing this doctorate?"

What is a doctorate?

We conceived of and wrote this book primarily for readers who have already started on their part-time doctorate or for those who are about to embark on this exciting next step. However, we know that some of our readers will have picked the book up in order to help you consider whether a part-time doctorate is the right choice for you. For this reason we wanted to give some consideration to the different types of doctorates that are available, and their purpose and features. Additionally, we wanted to support you to understand the variety of other paths part-time researchers follow and what you might share in common, or what might be different, about your own experience.

A doctorate is any advanced higher education qualification that leads to a doctoral degree, and therefore conveys upon you the personal title "Doctor." We use "advanced" in this context to mean that a doctorate would not usually be your first degree and for this reason can sometimes be referred to as a "postgraduate degree" because anyone undertaking it would have already graduated (at least) once. A masters degree is also a postgraduate degree, by this same reasoning, but is not a doctorate. This point of potential confusion in terminology is not the only confusing label that exists when we are talking about doctorates. Thus in the first part of this chapter we aim to help you to gain some clarity of names and terms, and to understand your options. As neither of us are historians, and as you are unlikely to be consulting this book for reasons of historical research, we don't want to take you on a tour of the origins and proliferation of types of doctorates across the globe. We will instead focus here on the most common types of doctorates that you might encounter, and in doing this we make the assumption that you are considering your own options for personal, professional, or career development, or for the application of your professional expertise in practice to an academic qualification. This means we will offer you practical information that you can use to make informed choices about engaging with doctoral study. The doctorate has evolved greatly since its original emergence as a teaching qualification, and later a professorial apprenticeship, and it has diversified to accommodate and include different types of researchers, and different types of professionals, with different educational backgrounds and career contexts (Jones, 2018). You have a lot of choice, and so it pays to be informed.

An umbrella term

The PhD (Doctor of Philosophy, sometimes also called the DPhil in some UK contexts) is the most common type of doctorate, but it is far from being the only type of doctorate. Professional doctorates such as the EdD (Doctorate in Education), doctorates by publication, the Doctor of Fine Arts or of Performing Arts, and industrial doctorates have also been created to shape the doctoral level qualification to the needs of different industries. It is for this reason we have used the term "doctorate" throughout this book, to ensure we refer to and include all researchers who are undertaking doctorates. In defining this, it is pertinent to also mention that we have chosen also to use the term "researcher" to describe you, the people who are undertaking doctorates. This is because people undertaking doctorates may be university staff or students, or indeed both at the same time. A doctorate may be undertaken by a full-time university staff member who is studying part-time. An alternative scenario is that a full- or part-time student may be engaged in teaching work, the terms and conditions of which relate to university staff. In some European countries all doctoral researchers are classed as staff regardless of their teaching status. There is a longstanding and ongoing debate concerning the staff-or-student status of doctoral researchers (see for example Else, 2017), and therefore their rights and responsibilities as members of the academic community. It is good to be aware of this, and to check your own status, rights, and responsibilities as a researcher in the country and institution at which you are studying, or considering studying at.

A research degree

Whatever your doctorate type, and whatever your status as a researcher, in order to gain your doctorate you will be expected, over a period of several years, to engage in novel research to produce a significant body of scholarly work that makes an original contribution to the existing knowledge in your field. A doctorate is often therefore referred to as a "research degree," which is reflected in our choice of the "researcher" terminology, discussed previously. In many institutions doctoral researchers may be referred to by the synonym "postgraduate researchers" (see also "doctoral scholars," though this is more common in the arts, humanities and social sciences). Because all doctorates are "research degrees," they can often be thought of purely as a research challenge, awarded on completion of a substantial research project. However, completing the research project and generating data or new insight is not the entirety of the challenge of a doctorate. The examined end product of a doctorate commonly includes a research thesis, or dissertation, a written and bound volume documenting your "original contribution to knowledge." The word "thesis" is related in its origins to the word "proposition" or "something put forth" and the word "dissertation" stems from words such as "discuss" and "examine." These ideas bring us closer to the concept of the doctorate. The degree is awarded to those who research a given topic, and then present a written proposition, or argument, in which their chosen topic is discussed and examined at length. A doctoral thesis can take different formats and be different lengths depending on the type of doctorate you are doing, but is a long-form document that not only records what you have done, but tells the story of your research, its origins and how it was conceived, why it is relevant, how it was done and by whom, and what it means for the field. This level of scholarship, of critical thinking, and of argument construction is part of the "essence" of the doctorate. However, it certainly isn't the whole essence of the doctorate. Whilst we have previously described the outcome, or the product, of the doctorate, this book primarily focuses on the process. Becoming 'doctorly' is a process of development, or identity shift, professional learning, and personal growth. It is a process as well as a product, and that nature of that process should be revisited regularly as you progress (Wellington, 2013). It's a journey of discovery about yourself as much as about your topic area, and only you can decide for yourself what the essence of your doctorate will be.

A route into an academic career?

One common reason for beginning a doctorate is that it is a natural progression on an academic pathway, an opportunity to reach higher and to succeed at the pinnacle of academic qualifications. Often, people begin doctoral study after having enjoyed engaging with research work through a masters degree. It should be noted though that the requirement for a masters degree before doing your doctorate varies by discipline, and by university. Different country contexts also influence this; for example in Australia, a doctorate may require you to secure a masters degree if you haven't already graduated with an Australian honours degree (which includes a fourth "research" year). In North America, doctoral programmes often include a masters-level first year involving coursework and examinations as part of the package.

However you arrive at your doctorate, avoid making assumptions about what will happen post-doctorate. Most doctorate holders *do not* work in academic industries, even though most people in academic careers *do* hold doctorates. In most countries that award doctorates, holding a doctoral research degree qualifies the holder to teach at university level in the degree's specific field. However, it should be noted that holding a doctoral degree is not always a requirement of securing an academic or faculty position in all universities. A range of alternative experiences and qualifications may provide the necessary professional expertise and credibility in some disciplines and university institutions. If an academic career is your goal, there may be other ways to achieve that goal. Additionally, the number of opportunities to maintain an academic career long term are far fewer than the number of doctoral graduates year on year. Academia is a very competitive career field with high levels of job precarity. Securing a permanent academic post requires a great deal of forward planning, network building, CV building, and not a small amount of luck. If this is your goal, the activities throughout this book will help you think through how to build these into your doctoral journey. Similarly, if you have no academic aspirations following the doctorate and see this as a journey in and of itself, that is perfectly OK.

A contextualised experience

The notion of what a doctorate is, how it proceeds, what it includes, what constitutes success, and therefore how it is experienced and valued by the researchers who undertake it, varies across geographical location and with the conventions of the different disciplines. Additionally, prior study experience, and current professional experience, identity, and mindset will flavour the doctoral experience. Becoming "a student" again, and adopting a novice role after a period of relative seniority or authority within a professional context, creates uncertainty (Haegele, 2022) and requires some conscious navigation and empathetic supervisors. The experience is also influenced by the core mission and values of the university hosting the degree – universities have working cultures, as is the case for any large organisation. For example, a university that has a strong commitment to creating social impact may reflect this in the way they encourage doctoral researchers to engage with the wider issues of society. A university that centres on upholding traditional notions of knowledge and discovery will tend to bring a more theoretically grounded flavour to the opportunities they offer doctoral researchers. A university dedicated to maximising graduate employability may present more of a focus on the development of core skills and competencies through the doctorate. Your choice of institution can impact your experience as much as your choice of mode, topic, and supervisor(s). It is within your power to find out more before you commit. If you can, talk to the existing doctoral students, meet with potential supervisors, and visit the department and university campus before you make your selection.

Types of part-time doctorates

A part-time doctorate offers flexibility and opens up opportunities for thousands of people every year who cannot or do not want to be constrained by a full-time study model. The range of reasons for seeking this flexibility in approach are widely varied. It may make financial sense to work and study in parallel and of course may be the only practical option for some students, especially if you are self-funded. Part-time study can better accommodate an ongoing career, with your research and practice complementing and enhancing each other. A part-time doctorate can be an accessible route for people with caring responsibilities or community commitments. In our careers we have spoken to part-time researchers who prioritise balance in their life and enjoy a part-time pace to their study, researchers who are combining a part-time doctorate with a bid to represent their country in a national sporting team, and researchers who are in very senior roles (for example in clinical or broadcasting careers) who want to make the doctorate fit in and around their high-profile and demanding work.

It can be tempting to consider the only difference between part-time and full-time doctorates to boil down to the amount of time you are allocated to complete the course. Whilst it may constitute part-time hours in terms of official working patterns, it also offers the opportunity for full-time thinking. There are challenges in this, in sustaining momentum and motivation, in staying on your supervisor(s) "radar" and building your professional networks. PhD researchers, studying part-time within a full-time model, may experience difficulties of access to resources and communities that students in professional doctoral programmes that are constructed for part-time study do not (Gardner and Gopaul, 2012). Recent findings also suggest that part-time PhD students are motivated by the opportunity to advance knowledge and build scholarly relationships with others, yet their access to scholarly communities can be limited, and may lead to demotivation and the formation of assumptions regarding their and their supervisor's roles and the overall purpose of their doctoral education (Turner, 2021). Yet the same study also showed that part-time students reported higher levels of satisfaction than did full-time students. As such, this book supports you to anticipate and plan for such challenges. There are also many additional reasons why you might prefer to approach your doctorate part-time, such as the extended maturation time for your research. Use this to your advantage by recognising the benefits of engaging with more flexible, dispersed, and varied patterns of working on your doctoral project. As you progress through this book you will find many stories of researchers who have done just that, and greatly value their part-time experience.

In the following section we give a brief overview of some of the most common types of part-time doctorates. We have kept the details here intentionally brief due to the great variety in structure, eligibility, and submission criteria. There are no universal models that apply to these doctorate types across all nationality contexts, or even across all institutions within a particular country. It is important for aspiring doctoral researchers to properly investigate the terms and conditions they are entering into. For this reason, we repeat our advice to you – look closely at the details of each opportunity you come across, in considering the best option for you.

A **part-time PhD** simply describes the doing of a PhD at a reduced pace, with fewer hours per week. How part-time this is, your working pattern, and therefore your overall time to completion, is agreed by a process of negotiation between you, your supervisor(s), your university, and your funder (if applicable), each of who will have preferences and limitations. This option will usually incur the same costs in terms of tuition fees, albeit spread out over the longer period of time.

A whole cluster of specialist degree types fall into the **professional doctorate** category. For example, taking a focus on education (EdD), clinical psychology (DClinPsy), architecture (DArch), business administration (DBA), engineering (EngD), and many other specialist titles. Whilst now common in the USA, UK (Mellors-Bourne et al., 2016), and Australia, universities in continental Europe and elsewhere in the world tend not to have adopted this form of the doctoral programme (Haegele, 2022; Hawkes and Yerrabati, 2018). The EdD (specifically in the UK and USA contexts) is the most studied of these professional pathways comprising more than 60 per cent of the research into professional doctorates (Hawkes and Yerrabati, 2018).

Professional doctorates are awarded to individuals who research practice in their own specialist field. They are directed at mid-career professionals in specific industries or career pathways and are intended to operate in parallel with that existing career, with researchers completing the doctorate as a career development opportunity. As with all doctorates they involve original research and the production of a scholarly thesis, but they tend to offer additional specialised training in the form of assessed courses that facilitate the building of research skills and practices in the early phases. A professional doctorate may be commonly presented (by those who design them) as a more tailored "next generation" alternative to the "traditional" doctorate (Green, Maxwell, and Shanahan, 2001). Yet professional doctorates can vary greatly. Additionally, more traditional doctorates (e.g. the PhD) have been adapted in many institutions to accommodate practice-based methodologies and assessment modes (Hughes and Tight, 2013), and so careful investigation of exactly what is and is not on offer to you as a prospective learner is warranted.

An **industrial doctorate** is offered by some universities. It is an opportunity for people currently in employment as a researcher (usually in the engineering or biotechnology industries) to undertake a focused research project that is co-supervised by their employer and an academic supervisory team, allowing candidates to achieve a PhD while remaining in their existing industry role. It can look similar to a professional doctorate in engineering (EngD) but takes a PhD project format rather than involving the coursework stages of the professional doctorate.

We are seeing the steady emergence of specialist doctorates designed specifically to encourage the production of a substantial creative work (a composition, performance, or novel for example) prior to or alongside a scholarly thesis. This type of doctorate – a **creative or fine arts doctorate** (practice as research) – often combines the early taught elements of the professional doctorate with the requirement to produce and critique a creative piece via submission of a thesis that contextualises and analyses the performance practice in relation to the research literature.

The **PhD by publication** (which also may be known by titles such as a thesis by publication, or a doctorate by published works) is awarded to a researcher who has carried out extensive research over a significant period of time and who has achieved a number of publications in high-quality journals. The exact time period, timing of the publications, number and type of publications, or criteria related to co-authorship may vary between institutions. This doctorate is generally awarded to those who produce a doctoral thesis that includes these collected works and demonstrates a coherent scholarly narrative linking them together into a novel argument. The choice to pursue this route prospectively (generating publications as you move through the PhD) will be influenced by the necessity of holding research publications for success in your future chosen career route. For existing academics who are already publishing work, the benefits of this pathway (retrospective collation of pre-existing publications) are that it provides access to achieving a doctorate via publications generated through existing workload, rather than creating additional workload in the form of a dissertation (Jackson, 2013). For a full contemporary picture of the PhD by publication, and to read narratives written by researchers who have undertaken this route, please see Chong and Johnson (2022).

An **online doctorate** (doctorate at a distance) can describe a range of programmes or situations. The term includes both PhDs and professional doctorates that make use of a predominantly online platform for any taught elements, professional development elements, supervision meetings, and cohort-building activities. An online doctorate may be purposefully designed as a globally dispersed cohort approach, or remote technologies and approaches may be used as a way to stay connected throughout a part-time PhD. Using online modes enables the inclusion of researchers in different geographical locations and global contexts bringing advantages such as enriched conversations, challenge to parochial attitudes, and the building of strong cross-cultural bonds (Wildy et al., 2015), as well as the challenge of staying connected to a distant and commonly temporally offset research community. Even if not permanently based "remotely," increasing numbers of doctoral researchers now study "at a distance" and therefore rarely attend a physical campus, perhaps due to working patterns or periods of travel for data collection. A cautionary point is offered to us by Dowling and Wilson (2017), whose study demonstrated the need for additional time to research and gain confidence with the right digital tools, and to secure the supervisor buy-in and digital familiarity needed to craft a productive remote-working partnership. A forthcoming volume in this series by McChesney et al. will be useful to explore if you are planning to study for a doctorate at a distance.

Having read about the options, you may have some questions. Are you thinking: What's right for me? What if I choose the wrong mode? Can I change to a different degree type midway? If I start part time can I move to full time, or vice versa? If I have already published in the course of my doctorate, might I be better to shift to a PhD by publication? Are all doctorates equal in their status, reputation, and academic rigour? The answers to these questions, as you will expect from what you have learned in this chapter so far, are complex. In almost all cases it depends on country and disciplinary conventions, any prerequisites you need to have in place, and the availability of places on the degree type you want to move into, as well as on university and funder regulations. Always check with your institution; do not assume your right to make programme changes. Remember that being classed a student rather than a member of staff may change what policies and laws guide your rights and responsibilities. If you are wondering what option to choose, the following two real world reflections and the two reader activities might bring you some way closer to making a decision.

Real-world reflection – choosing the right degree for me

The "real world reflection" presented below has been adapted from a blog post written by Jon, one of the authors of this book, as he began his part-time doctorate in 2014. He compares his options – the PhD? Or the EdD?

> I was put in the enviable position of being able to choose between an EdD and a part-time PhD at the same institution and on the same topic, so really this left little to choose from other than the model of delivery. As I worked through my choices and came up with pros and cons for each, neither option seemed to race ahead from the other in my thinking. The two main benefits I saw in the EdD are the presence of a cohort for informal support, and the structure to help retain focus during a part-time doctorate. The EdD would have a shorter thesis but with several assessed formal assignments in the first three years. The PhD has a longer thesis, but no early formal assignments. In the EdD I would be part of a cohort all starting the

journey together, whereas in a PhD I would be likely to be one of a much smaller number in the department. What shaped my final choice of a part-time PhD, was me and my own background and circumstances. I talked to several academics who helped me to see that much of the work I have been doing over the last few years has been developing the practices I need for doctoral study, that is, reading around my areas of interest, engaging with theory, attending conferences, and building support networks. Building these practices is the purpose of the early phase of the EdD. Given that I have already begun this journey, some of the scaffolding offered by the EdD might then feel slightly restrictive and delay the start of the data collection phase of my research. By considering the EdD, however, I have become aware of those parts of the training model that may be lacking in the PhD, and the gaps I will need to fill for myself, such as creating the support network that a cohort would provide.

We are happy to report that having completed the part-time PhD, Jon was happy with his choice. We stress that neither option is better. Choose the one that is the best fit for you, and the stage you are at, with the skills and experiences and networks you have.

Activity: What's on my doctoral wish list?

This simple starter activity will support you if you are at the stage of choosing your best-fit doctorate type. In response to each of the following statements, answer yes or no. For those to which you answer yes, ask yourself why you feel this way, how you can verify your understanding, and where appropriate, if this is a "must have" or if you might consider other options.

In all cases, think back to the information that we have shared so far in this chapter and be wary of making assumptions about yourself or about the rules of your university, the application process, potential supervisor(s), course fees, funding, or the involvement of your employer. We encourage you to make direct enquiries about any of these things, and indeed any other questions you may have before enrolling in a doctorate.

- There is a specific university I want to attend
- There is a specific department I want to join
- There is a specific supervisor I want to work with
- There is a specific research question I want to answer
- I need to have a master's degree to be eligible for my chosen course
- I need to have an established career or practice to be eligible for my chosen course
- I would benefit from the taught elements of a professional doctorate
- I have significant experience as a researcher
- I am confident that I have enough publications to enrol on a doctorate by published work
- I would require funding to enable me to complete a doctorate
- My employer would fund my doctorate

Wouldn't it be great if by asking you the preceding questions we could accurately model the option that would suit you best by plugging your answers into a doctorate matching algorithm? Of course, in reality, this is not possible because the preceding is just part of who you are, and your best fit is a function of many more contextual factors. We offer this activity simply as a point for reflection, and encourage you to talk to current part-time doctoral researchers, potential supervisors, other academic staff, family, and friends in order to make your choice. This chapter's second real-world reflection follows, and may supplement your thinking.

Real-world reflection – gaining recognition for my contribution

This reflection has been adapted from two blog posts on thrivingparttime.com by **Dr Karen Campbell**, an educational development researcher who completed her PhD by publication at Glasgow Caledonian University in 2020. You can connect with her on Twitter @karencampbellWP.

If you are an expert in your field with a significant portfolio of publications under your belt or are working towards developing such a portfolio, why not complete a PhD by publication? Publishing from a doctoral thesis has always been an implicit expectation and this route allows both the successful completion of the doctorate and your publishing objectives to be achieved. The process allows people who have not followed the traditional route towards a

PhD to obtain recognition for their contribution and the subject knowledge they have developed throughout their career. Thus, it widens participation to doctoral level study. For me, the PhD by publication provided a framework, a way forward from which I could map out a path to submission. The publication route to a doctorate is essentially about meta-analysis. It's about abstracting yourself from the micro-level of your work and considering the macro themes emerging in your publications. I took a prospective approach and worked to produce and publish academic papers around my area of work with a view to the end goal of a PhD. The advantage here (over the retrospective route which recognises works you have published previously) is that this forward planning provides you with a clear focused narrative for your research outputs. It's worth bearing in mind, though, that you may not be automatically linked into support mechanisms available to those undertaking more traditional full-time routes – the help, advice, networks, and resources available may differ significantly. Doing a PhD by publication can be isolating, and I built my own support network. I've heard it said that the PhD by publication route is much shorter than the traditional one, but I beg to differ. Consider the time required to complete the research, write it up into draft papers, submit these, address reviewer feedback, and publish. Then there's the time I needed to reflect on the thesis' originality, coherence, and contribution as a whole to the body of knowledge.

I had to develop my thesis research question and plan and write my critical review of the literature. The process also required me to show the impact of my research and so must include a significant element of application and reflection on this in practice; something else to factor in terms of time. Overall, though, I gained a lot of new skills, and have greatly developed as a researcher. My publications have increased and have become more varied. My confidence and my academic profile has grown.

Adapted from: https://thrivingparttime. com/2021/03/22/what-is-a-phd-by-publication/ and https://thrivingparttime. com/2021/03/29/phd-by-publication-because-the-whole-is-greater-than-the-sum-of-the-parts/

Managing the costs

To finance your studies, you may choose to work part time or full time, you may be sponsored by your employer, or you may be seeking a doctoral student loan or to apply for funding from a university, a government-funded research council or organisation, a charity, a professional body, or a scholarly society. The landscape for doctoral funding is yet another area of complexity to be navigated and may change from year to year. We advise you to check all funding criteria carefully to ensure you are eligible before spending a large chunk of your time on an application or proposal. If you will be applying for funding together with a supervisor, do discuss the sources to which you might apply, their expectations of you during and after the doctorate, and the terms and conditions they will apply (for example some sources may limit the amount of paid work you can engage in, or limit you to full-time–only study). Ask also about the success rates for applicants for each funding source you are applying for, noting that it may take a few attempts to gain the funding for your doctorate, and so it is always best to be prepared for this.

Weighing up your options, managing the costs and seeking the benefits involved, and assessing the balance of potential risks and anticipated gains is part of any career decision. Choosing whether or not to do a doctorate is no different. The value that a doctorate brings to you, both as a process of in-depth learning, and as an opportunity for career development or consolidation, is a function of choosing the right opportunities and options for you. Throughout this book we bring you first-hand accounts of the many positives, benefits, and gains others have experienced as well as sharing copious ideas and tools that will help you to avoid, avert, or navigate the challenges you will face. We intend that the stories, ideas, and activities we share will help you to make sense of your own best fit and bring to you a sense of agency and empowerment in how you interact with challenging times. We also suggest that a clarity of purpose for your doctorate can be achieved by setting realistic expectations and reminding yourself of the positive value of doctoral study. This will help you to encourage yourself and help you to sustain motivation as you progress. We invite you to begin the process by considering what is motivating you to seek out or succeed with doctoral study, at whatever point you are at in your journey today.

Activity: What is motivating me to begin doctoral study?

This activity asks you to react to the following list of potential personal motivations for completing a doctorate and find those that resonate with you. Consider each in turn, answering either "Yes," "No," or "I don't know" – there are no right or wrong answers. Keep a note of those you feel most strongly connected to, and revisit them when you want to refresh your sense of purpose.

- I like to challenge myself
- It is important to me to leave a legacy
- I aspire to an academic career
- The opportunity to be creative excites me
- I want others to feel proud of me
- I would enjoy using the title of "Doctor"
- I want to feel connected to sites of new knowledge and learning
- My promotion or next career move depends on it
- I want to be first in my family to achieve a doctorate
- I am excited to be part of a scholarly community
- I would like to stay connected to my university
- I want to increase my professional credibility
- I am keen to create a name for myself as an expert
- I would like to do something just for myself
- It is important to continue to improve my own knowledge and skills as a lifelong learner
- My research has the potential to help people
- I will enjoy the process of discovery
- I want to achieve the pinnacle of academic qualifications

- It appeals to me to prove that I can succeed
- Being part of a diverse global community inspires me
- I am inspired to do things differently than others in my profession
- I want to prove someone wrong about me

What else would you add to this list? What truly represents you?

Keeping a note of your motivations can help you to articulate your reasons to potential supervisors or funders in an application or interview situation too.

Each of the chapters that follow this one encourage you to reflect on your own situation. A doctorate is your personal journey, and the personal and professional value you draw down from it is yours to decide – you are the most important person in your doctorate. Indeed, as Wellington and Sikes (2006) point out, "biography is, and always will be, the crucial factor affecting perceptions and experiences" of a part-time doctorate. We hope you enjoy making your way through and reflecting on the insights we share.

Researchers recommend ...

- Focus on what you want from your doctorate, what opportunities, what structures, and what support. Thinking this through for yourself will help you to choose the best fit for you and to articulate it to others.

- Keep your eye on the positives but be ready for the challenges. Doctorates are a unique personal experience and require you to be proactive and demonstrate your personal agency.
- Anchor into your motivation for succeeding with the doctorate but be prepared for it to change as you gain new knowledge and understanding.

Where can I find out more?

The website https://doctoralresearchbydistance.wordpress.com/ and associated researcher community is an excellent resource for anyone working on their studies "'at a distance." Associated with this is a forthcoming book in the insider's guide series by Katrina McChesney, James Burford, Liezel Frick, and Tseen Khoo entitled *Doing Doctoral Research by Distance: Navigating Off-campus, Online, Hybrid, and Cross-national Doctoral Study*.

References

Chong, S. W., & Johnson, N. H. (Eds.). (2022) *Landscapes and Narratives of PhD by Publication, Demystifying Students' and Supervisors' Perspectives*. Switzerland: Springer Nature. Doi: 10.1007/978-3-031-04895-1

Dowling, R., & Wilson, M. (2017) Digital doctorates? An exploratory study of PhD candidates' use of online tools. *Innovations in Education and Teaching International*, 54:1, 76–86. doi: 10.1080/14703297.2015.1058720

Else, H. (2017) PhD students: time to make them university employees? *Times Higher Education*. Available at: https://www.timeshighereducation.com/news/phd-students-time-to-make-them-university-employees

Gardner, S. K., & Gopaul, B. (2012) The part-time doctoral student experience. *International Journal of Doctoral Studies*, 7:12, 63–78.

Green, B., Maxwell, T., & Shanahan, P. (Eds.). (2001) *Doctoral Education and Professional Practice: The Next Generation?* Armidale, NSW: Kardooair Press.

Haegele, D. (2022) *Joy and pain – a visit into scholarship: Managers' lived experience as part-time doctoral researchers*, PhD Thesis, University of Gliucestershire. doi: 10.13140/RG.2.2.25990.45129

Hawkes, D. & Yerrabati, S. (2018) A systematic review of research on professional doctorates. *London Review of Education*, 16:1, 10–27.

Hughes, C. & Tight, M. (2013) The metaphors we study by: the doctorate as a journey and/or as work. *Higher Education Research & Development*, 32:5, 765–775. doi: 10.1080/07294360.2013.777031

Jackson, D. (2013) Completing a PhD by publication: a review of Australian policy and implications for practice. *Higher Education Research & Development*, 32:3, 355–368. doi: 10.1080/07294360.2012.692666

Jones, M. (2018) Contemporary trends in professional doctorates. *Studies in Higher Education*, 43:5, 814–825. doi: 10.1080/03075079.2018.1438095

McChesney, K., Burford, J., Frick, L. & Khoo, T. (forthcoming) *Doing Doctoral Research by Distance: Navigating Off-campus, Online, Hybrid, and Cross-national Doctoral Study*. Abingdon: Routledge.

Mellors-Bourne, R., Robinson, C. & Metcalfe, J. (2016) *Provision of Professional Doctorates in English HE Institutions*. Cambridge: Careers Research and Advisory Centre.

Turner, H. A. (2021) I'm still valid: an explanatory sequential mixed-methods study of part-time PhD students' motivation and satisfaction. Electronic Theses and Dissertations. Paper 3592. doi: 10.18297/etd/3592

Wellington, J. (2013) Searching for 'doctorateness'. *Studies in Higher Education*, 38:1490–1503.

Wellington, J. & Sikes, P. (2006) "A doctorate in a tight compartment": why do students choose a professional doctorate and what impact does it have on their personal and professional lives? *Studies in Higher Education*, 31:723–734.

Wildy, H., Peden, S. & Chan, K. (2015) The rise of professional doctorates: case studies of the doctorate in education in China, Iceland and Australia, *Studies in Higher Education*, 40:5, 761–774. doi: 10.1080/03075079.2013.842968

2 Drawing your map

By the end of this chapter you will

- Understand that there are many visible and hidden parts of the curriculum to navigate.
- Be able to identify your personal goals and what support you need to achieve these.
- Understand what people value about their doctorates and how to develop this as part of your journey.

What's in store

The comparatively unstructured nature of the doctorate and the nature of doing original research with no pre-destined outcomes can be both liberating and disorientating. In this chapter we draw upon reflections and observations collected from part-time researchers, who share their important moments of realisation as well as stories of how they navigated their doctoral journeys. We hope you will find these stories informative and reassuring, as you consider your own personalised journey through the doctorate. Using structured activities to prompt you to consider your own personal wish lists and preferences, we will support you to begin your own

DOI : 10.4324/9781003223931-3

realistic road map for the doctorate and to plan for your future development with an appreciation of all the opportunities that will be open to you.

Navigating a doctorate

It can be a common, and in fact hindering, misconception that once you begin your doctorate, you are on a specific course of scheduled activity that sets out, guides, monitors, and measures your pathway to completion and provides you with all the resources you will need to succeed. Your experiences of previous courses of study at bachelor's or master's level might lead you to make the assumption that you are entering into a structured, modular course, where subject experts will be assigned to guide, facilitate, and quality assure your learning journey and will create an exciting and developmental curriculum for study. Operating on this assumption, and therefore waiting for "things to start," or expecting to be advised about what to do next, or assuming that your academic colleagues have their eye on your progress and will keep you on track, can be the source of much consternation. It can also lead to feelings of disorientation and frustration for doctoral researchers, and in hindsight it can create a feeling that your time has been wasted. This is because the doctorate generally expects quite a different mode of engagement from you. Doing your own original research, and finding out the previously unknown, is an inherently uncertain process involving some unchartered territory and through which there is often not one right way to navigate. Rather than following a predestined route mapped out for you, it requires you to draw your own metaphorical "route map," charting the course as you go.

We will refer to the idea of "your map" throughout this chapter, and in doing this we are attempting to capture the concept of a reflective tool or visual aid that helps you to understand the doctoral process and your learning journey through it. For some readers, creating a visual map or diagram for yourself may be something you find value in. For others, making mental notes, lists, or just considering the ideas and noticing what resonates with you may be preferred. Do engage with this chapter however you choose. A key skill of all doctoral researchers is navigating the journey in a way that works best for you, and for part-time doctorates, this can be even more complex to get to grips with. There may be more elements for you to consider and knit together as a part-time researcher, and the more gradual pace of study may mean that there are longer pauses in progress, or more restrictions on your time. Studying part-time can also give you more thinking time to reflect and make sense of the doctoral landscape and your route through it.

The metaphor of a journey can be contrasted with a metaphor of the doctorate as work (Hughes and Tight, 2013). One of the participants in our recent workshops for part-time doctoral researchers described the process.

> I think of my PhD like freelance work. Yes, you are responsible for making your own motivation, and impetus for getting the work done, you bring your own style, expertise, and values and ultimately you are responsible for the success of the project, and for delivering it on time. But you have to work with different people like supervisors, collaborators, advisors, committees, administrators, and even other organisations to get that work done. You are responsible, but you can't do it alone, you need

to know how the different systems work, and get the right backing and introductions to get things done. I did not realise at the outset how much navigating and negotiating I would have to get involved in. Or that it's my job to secure that introduction, or that permission. Do not wait to be offered what you need, go and ask for it.

Most types of doctorates will generally provide you with a somewhat less directive framework than any previously experienced taught courses. Depending on your degree type, you may experience some structured elements in the earlier stages. Perhaps your course will even offer an initial taught phase that is designed to prepare you for an independent study phase. Or for creative arts doctorates there can be a "creative phase" followed by a "critical phase" that involves the production of a single thesis or multiple scholarly arguments. A PhD, or PhD by publication, may provide you with less scaffolding still, in that it requires you to engage with reading, researching, and writing as self-managed parallel processes from the outset. These shifts – masters-to-doctorate, taught-to-independent, creative-to-critical – can come as a stark change of skill set and mindset to the researchers who undertake them. All the different formats for a doctorate have one thing in common, though: There is no one right way to complete them. There is no set pathway, and no right series or sequence to follow that will lead you to success. Assuming that there is a "right way" can be a barrier to progress.

In leading many workshops for part-time researchers on the topic of navigating a personal journey through the doctorate, we have commonly created and compared different photographs or drawings of "pathways." We use these images metaphorically, to prompt reflection. This helps researchers to articulate the journey they assumed they would experience, to define the journey they are actually taking part in, and to support each other to reconcile the difference between the two and readjust their expectations. For example, during our workshops we give newly enrolled doctoral researchers the option to select an image that represents "the journey to come." They will usually choose something like the image in Figure 2.1, and in discussing their reasons for choosing such a photograph, researchers commonly communicate their understanding that they are on a path that goes from one place to another, with a fixed start and end point "to be revealed." The path, whilst meandering, is clearly visible and has been trodden before. They acknowledge that there will be "ups and downs" to the journey with progress at some points being more difficult than others.

But if we run this activity with researchers who are midway through the doctorate, the choice of image

Figure 2.1 A typical pathway representing perceptions of the doctoral journey

Photo by Lili Popper on Unsplash

changes. Many will acknowledge that the pathway they had imagined is not as visible, as fixed in destination, or as linear as they imagined it would be. Workshop participants in this phase may choose a photograph something more like the two example Figures 2.2 and 2.3, perhaps showing an obscured path indicating they feel "off track" or "lost," or describing their experience of feeling like they are creating a new path for the very first time. Or they may reflect on an image with many converging paths, destination options, and implicit rules, to metaphorically describe their real-world journey.

Taking time to consciously realign expectations with reality, and the letting go of old ideas and assumptions, can bring you a much-needed opportunity to make sense of your circumstances and experiences to date.

Figure 2.2 An obscured pathway that must be located or created

Photo by Klemen Tušar on Unsplash

Figure 2.3 Convergent and interweaving multi-lane
pathways

Photo by Denys Nevozhai on Unsplash

Honing your map-making skills

One assumption that *will* serve you well in your quest,
however, is that this process of navigating as you go,
and traversing your own journey, is not beyond you. You
are an accomplished decision-maker. You have already
made several important decisions related to navigating
your doctorate in your own way, by choosing to study
part time. You are likely to have considered the mode, the
topic, suitable timings, and the right location for your doctoral work based on your own knowledge of the interests
that you have, what you hope to gain from the process in
terms of career enhancement or personal fulfilment, and
in the context of how you prefer to engage with the work

of doctoral study considering other factors that make you uniquely you. You've got this!

Doing a doctorate brings an opportunity to spend time investigating your chosen areas of interest in great detail. Your doctoral education will involve immersion in your topic area as you become an expert in your field. It will also support you to gain advanced research skills, as you engage with the practicalities of gathering, analysing, and reporting your findings. Further, your powers of scholarly critique and argument construction will be shaped through the process of writing supported by peer review and feedback. Additionally, your part-time doctorate can be an opportunity not only to develop knowledge and skills related to your research area but to also explore the different professional development opportunities open to you as part of your degree, and offered to you by your department, university, or wider professional networks. The doctoral landscape is rich with opportunities to learn about how to engage well with academic life, how to succeed in a range of careers, and to consider the factors that help research to reach a wider audience and spark societal impact or influence.

Considering all of these opportunities in light of both your current professional knowledge and your aspirations for after the doctorate can help you understand how to prioritise the wealth of learning opportunities, events, networks, and spaces open to you. Reflecting on where you would like your doctorate to take you and your professional expertise post graduation, will help you to select and prioritise the right development opportunities for you. One thing is clear, you can't do them all!

In order to begin, or to reshape, your doctoral "route map" we would like to offer you the opportunity to consider what brought you to this learning journey and any experiences you'd like to have or outcomes of your doctorate you would like to see come to fruition by the time it is completed. Thinking ahead like this, or Beginning with the End in Mind (Covey, 1989), helps you to align your motivation for starting your doctorate with what will sustain you through it and what will motivate you to finish it. By doing this we invite you to consider the kind of added value you want to seek from the process.

Adding value to your doctorate

Doctoral graduates derive many benefits from their time studying and you can expect these "value-added" components to have an impact in a number of areas such as your career success, long-term friendships, skills and competencies, and even your personal identity (Bryan and Guccione, 2018). Through in-depth interviews with doctoral graduates, Bryan and Guccione also reported the positive impact of succeeding with a doctorate on how graduates viewed themselves and their place in a globally connected world. Importantly, in light of what we have already discussed in this chapter, this model of the value of a doctorate strongly suggests that what constitutes value-added is personal to each individual. Whether you see value and how much value you see in something depends on your uniquely individual situation. For some, the value of your doctorate will take the form of new learning, greater comprehension of a complex issue, and sharpened critical thinking. Others will be motivated by engaging with opportunities to gain experiences or career opportunities or to acquire new skills and techniques. Yet others will thrive within the formation of professional and personal relationships, including new disciplinary communities as well as friendships that enable psychological and social support and transcend the doctoral period. The value of your doctorate lies in your ability to draw down what you need based on your circumstances, learning needs, career preferences, and personal wish list.

One point that it will be useful to note is that the doctoral graduates from Bryan and Guccione's research reported that they had proactively chosen to seek out and engage with development opportunities, and that choosing the right development activities required them to consciously reflect on what they needed and wanted. The following activity supports you with this, asking you to consider why you are here in your part-time doctorate and what will enable you at the end to say that it was worth doing.

Activity: What will make my doctorate worthwhile?

We recognise that for some readers this may be the first time you are considering the ideas presented in this chapter; for others this may be something you have put a great deal of thought into over the last few months or years. Whatever stage you are at, try to approach this activity with an open mind. Consider what you want and what is important to you, not what you feel you should want, or what others want from you. Answer the following questions as honestly as you can. Expect that you will find some of the questions difficult to answer and try to be comfortable with any questions that generate further unknowns. By defining what you don't yet know, you will be able to focus on the answers you need to seek. Whilst this sounds quite like a mystical mantra, it actually refers to Clarkson and Gilbert's (1991) application of the ideas of (un)conscious (in)competence, a framework that describes a process of gradual learning and the need for a flexible open mindedness as you build awareness of your developing expertise.

The work you produce in this activity, and indeed throughout this book, will only be seen by you, unless you choose to share it. If you want, you may share any of your insights with the Thriving Part-Time support community on social media using #ThrivingPartTime or on our blog.

This activity asks you to consider what motivated you to embark on this journey and to think ahead to the end of your studies and consider the factors that will enable you to say it has been a success. It also supports you to consider how you might reach those desired outcomes. This will be personal to you, so please respond to the following questions (using the prompts that follow them if you like) in any way you find meaningful, for example brainstorming keywords or concepts, mind-mapping, writing in full sentences, creating a mood board, audio recording your reflections, or drawing your responses.

What led you to begin your doctorate?
What did you envision it would be like?
What were the learning opportunities or lifestyle elements that you sought?
What benefits did you anticipate?

What are your hopes for your doctorate?
How will your experience enrich your professional, social, community, family, or personal life?

What assumptions may you have made about your journey through the doctorate?
How will you go about resetting these?

What are the biggest unknowns for you at this stage?
Are any of them getting in the way of your progress?

What conditions help you to be at your best?
What environmental factors, opportunities, supporting structures, or relationships will sustain you through this journey?

What comes after your doctorate?
Where is your thinking right now?
Will you do the same job, a new job, or perhaps take up a new career path, a career break, or retirement?
Has your goal changed from when you started?
Do you feel you have more options now, or fewer?

Who do you need to talk to now?
Are there people you want to inform, discuss or negotiate any of the preceding answers with?

Before moving into the next section, consider what you have just outlined and note if there are any specific areas of knowledge, resources, permissions, or colleagues that you need to help you achieve this. Your reflections could involve seeking out supervisory support (see Chapter 4) or the support of others, which you can think more about in Chapter 7.

Real-world reflection – an integrated approach

I can honestly say that doing my PhD part time was the right decision for me. My reasons for choosing part time were largely financial. I was already working as an administrator at my university when I considered postgraduate research and was able to register as a staff candidate, where I paid no tuition fees but received no stipend. Not having a stipend meant that I needed paid work alongside my PhD to pay the rent. For the first couple of years, I stayed in my university administration job, which gave me valuable insights into the inner workings of academic life and "how things get done" in a university. From there, I was fortunate to get a position as a part-time research associate on various projects in different departments. This was not without its challenges; getting up to speed with entirely different bodies of literature was difficult, and it meant needing to juggle my time and other commitments, although this worked in my favour too. For instance, I once switched to working full time as a research associate for a month so I could submit a report on time, but then took the next month off in lieu to work on my PhD. Working on projects alongside my PhD was overwhelmingly positive. It gave me experience of working in multidisciplinary teams, applying my methodological skills to different fields, writing and publishing journal articles, and applying for grants.

So, while it may have taken twice as long to get my PhD than if I had done it full time, I was filling my CV along the way with the skills, experience, and achievements that I needed in order to secure an academic position. Doing those other jobs also gave me some helpful perspective on my PhD, in particular steering me away from any misguided notion that my PhD would ever be perfect. As a research associate, I frequently had tight deadlines where I had to submit a piece of work that I thought was good enough rather than perfect, and this definitely helped me when I approached the final stages of writing my PhD. I think my part-time paid work on other projects also helped to maintain my commitment to my PhD and meant that I never really got bored of it. Switching between my PhD and my paid work each week could be difficult, but on the whole, I think it helped me to stay focused and make the most of the time I did have to spend studying.

The preceding reflection from a part-time doctoral researcher in sociology illustrates an important point: That an integrated approach to managing different pieces of work, projects, workplaces, and research paradigms can be beneficial both to knowledge and to motivation. There are good points presented in the preceding account that relate to the successful journey through the doctorate and the ways in which "doctoral learning" occurs, which is worth us picking up for closer analysis here:

Firstly, the researcher in the preceding narrative shows us that taking part in "other research" supported them to grow as a researcher. They note that this learning concerned more than having access to new subject material. By working with interdisciplinary teams this individual came to appreciate their contribution as a specialist, and by applying their methodological knowledge in new ways they learned more about the possibilities and limitations of different approaches. Their experience gave them access to a range of activities that support research success and that are requirements of an academic career, such as funding capture and publishing. *New and relevant learning can happen informally outside "the project."*

Secondly, the individual in the preceding vignette shows us that succeeding in the doctorate requires more than a matter of subject knowledge and having time to do doctoral work. Motivation, focus, and enthusiasm come into play and understanding, managing, and cultivating these factors is required. *There are emotional psychological components to doctoral work and managing your relationship to your work is important*.

And thirdly, the account notes that the rhythms and habits of the doctoral journey matter and that they require careful consideration. Not just in the planning for busy times and deadlines, but in the weekly patterns of how you routinely make time and stick to it. *In keeping up momentum and enthusiasm for doctoral work there is value in forward planning and a flexible approach that builds in breaks and balance*.

Taken together, those points illustrate in practice the idea of the hidden curriculum of doctoral education (Elliot et al., 2020), that is, all of the unofficial channels of genuine and useful learning that can be acquired by doctoral researchers. This informal learning can take place both within and outside of the physical and metaphorical boundaries of academia, and it can take place in many different ways, in various spaces, and be supported by a range of players. The hidden curriculum of the doctorate is a rich tapestry of insight that is relevant to disciplinary learning, cognitive processing and sensemaking, and meeting the psychological and emotional support the doctorate demands.

It takes more than academic thinking to navigate a doctorate

The preceding illustration of the motivational and emotional components of doctoral learning helps us to challenge another inhibiting assumption that can afflict new doctoral researchers – that the doctorate will be a purely cognitive, academic challenge. This idea is often reinforced by the reactions of colleagues, family, and friends, who good naturedly respond "Wow brainiac!" or "You must be really clever!" when you tell them you are entering into doctoral study. Whilst researchers are without doubt very intelligent people, the reason we want to challenge the idea that the doctorate is purely an academic test is that it can lead to unhelpful tendencies to try to solve feelings of being confused, stuck, stressed, or frustrated by "just studying harder." This in turn can cause an increase in frustration, as researchers find they cannot find just the right paper that will allow them to make sense of it all, or that they are putting in long hours, adding more and more information, and getting nowhere fast in terms of a visible product they are happy with.

This inability to self-solve the problem by just spending more time studying inevitably ends in stress, self-doubt, and even feelings of shame or inadequacy. When we feel this way, we tend to pull back from our colleagues and peers, isolate ourselves, avoid sharing our ideas or written work, or avoid the work altogether. Becoming isolated is a very easy trap to fall into in a doctorate, especially so for part-time researchers who are already more likely to be located away from peers, supervisors, and campus life. We want to strongly encourage you to avoid this thinking trap and to make time in your journey to consider the process, that is, *how* your doctoral work is getting done. In particular we encourage you to think about how informal interactions, social spaces, chance conversations with your peers, and regular checking in with your research network can help to unstick you when you are feeling stuck. Emotional and social support from others lessens the sense of isolation that affects so many of us in the pursuit of our doctorate (Cotterall, 2013) and is covered in some detail in Chapter 7. We recognise that for part-time doctoral researchers, creating regular spaces to come together with others takes more energy and advance planning, but we feel that it is worth all the effort and energy you can give to it. When you consider your own doctoral route map, consider alongside it the companions and contemporaries you will work with, support, commiserate with, and celebrate with along the way. The formal relationships that support you in navigating your doctorate are covered in much greater detail in Chapter 4, which looks at the complex task of effectively navigating supervisory support, and in Chapter 7, which takes a detailed look at how you can build supportive networks of people to help you make sense of and even enjoy the doctoral process. Your interactions with others, the psychological support, the listening ear, and the sense of validation and encouragement this can offer are key value-added opportunities offered by the hidden curriculum.

Elliot et al. (2020:11) put it very neatly:

> In this respect, our argument is that in the same way that the formal 'process' comprising supervision meetings, research seminars and conference participation is intended to guide doctoral researchers towards completion, i.e. the 'product', there are parallel, often invisible mechanisms (i.e. the hidden curriculum) that typically point to the informal 'process'. If given sufficient attention, their role is then better recognised – not to outshine but to complement, even reinforce – the formal curriculum provision, and in turn, bring together an enriched and strongly scaffolded doctoral learning experience.

Activity: Shaping your own part-time doctorate

In the following activity, we invite you to expand the journey metaphor and creatively capture a visual representation of your personalised route map through your own part-time doctorate. We suggest that as well as supporting your thinking and your "conscious competence" related to your doctorate, you might utilise the finished product as a visible reminder of why you are here, the progress you have made, and where you are heading. Again, approach this activity in the way that is most meaningful to you.

1. Start with the idea of a map or pathway. You might choose to draw this, select a photo from an image repository, audio describe it, build it in 3D from

modelling clay or building blocks, use mind-mapping software, or just close your eyes and mentally visualise it.

2. Begin to annotate your map. Acknowledge your point of entry into your part-time doctorate, your intended point of exit, the features of that journey along the way so far, and possibilities to come. These features might be specific landmarks that will help you to note your progress, vantage points that will enable you to see what is to come, or particular outcomes or outputs you are hoping to achieve. Include potential pitfalls that might delay you, steep climbs that will require you to give sustained effort, and sections of easy trekking. What are some of the opportunities and advantages that might occur that help you, and what are some of the challenges and obstacles you will need to overcome?

3. Now consider who your travelling companions are; the champions and cheerleaders who will travel with you. These people may be from your professional, academic, social, or family life. Are they with you throughout, or at specific points? Do you already know them, or will you need to recruit them? Add them to your map.

4. When do you hope to arrive at the different landmarks along the way? Are there deadlines you need to abide by? Have you factored in time to think, review, edit your plans, and redraft your writing? Have you made time for breaks, rest, and time away from the doctorate to make sure you stay balanced, well, and motivated? Add these notes to the map.

5. Well done! Your map is yours to share, revisit, and update as you go. Keep it in a safe place in your

office, computer, or mind. You might find coming back to this at the end of the book offers you a chance to add more landmarks and people you have not yet realised might be important to you.

Real-world reflection – my definition of success

The following reflection captures just one example of the messages we have hoped to convey throughout this chapter. That each doctorate will be initiated by different personal and professional motivations, and what counts as success, and value added – in this case the successful translation of research into professional practice, open-mindedness, increased professional networks, and career progression – is also a matter of context and perspective:

> Ultimately my career has involved doing many things at once, things that I enjoy, find interesting, and am passionate about. My PhD is but one strand to this, albeit a very significant strand. I have held three different full-time roles in the last few years since starting my part-time PhD, each a promotion or development opportunity, and each most definitely secured and enhanced by the developing skill set and network which can be traced back to my PhD. Now coming to the end of my PhD, my experience is that doing a doctorate is not a zero-sum qualification. But by doing a PhD you are

making yourself more informed, broad-minded, inquisitive, well-read, articulate, creative, and exposed to different people and cultures, and these are all skills and experiences I have found myself relying on in the last three years – as well as acquiring a greatly expanded professional network! At times though, I have needed to compartmentalise elements of my career. The views I express through academic pursuits as a researcher may earn me respect in one sphere and be accredited to my academic rigour and independence. Yet in another sphere this might ruffle feathers if I fail to toe the party line or speak in an unfamiliar language. It is upon me to navigate this translation process, and to conceive of how impact can be generated from my research findings without alienating me from my profession. There is much more to succeeding with the doctorate and getting what I wanted out of it than just completing a set course. But challenging as this may be, doing a part-time PhD is the best thing I have ever chosen to do. It has introduced me to some excellent people, fascinating conferences, and lifelong friends, and has shaped my life in ways I'm not sure would have happened otherwise.

Your doctorate is yours to own, and to shape. Your route to success is yours to map. This may change along the way, and that is to be expected, so enjoy the process of discovery. You can read more stories about the hidden curriculum of the doctorate and the learning journeys enabled through it at https://drhiddencurriculum.wordpress.com/.

Activity: How can I apply this to my own doctorate?

It may help to consolidate the ideas in this chapter by engaging with the following list-making activity. Quickly jot down your reflections, listing which of the points we have made that resonated with you. Aim for just three or four key learning points in each list.

List 1. How has this chapter confirmed what I already know?
List 2. How has this chapter challenged my thinking?
List 3. What new ideas will I keep in mind as I engage with my doctoral work?
List 4. What actions will I take as a result of reading this chapter?

Researchers recommend ...

- Consider what you want to gain from engaging with your part-time doctorate. Be honest with yourself about what you want. Whilst we don't operate in isolation, our own values, achievements, and hopes are what help to sustain motivation.
- Think carefully about the conditions that will help you to achieve the results you want. Avoid assumptions about how things "should" be done and communicate your ideas with those who can support you in achieving the challenges you set for yourself.
- Regularly revisit your "route map." The course may change, but that's to be expected, so stay agile.

References

Bryan, B., and Guccione, K. (2018) 'Was it worth it? A qualitative exploration of graduate perceptions of doctoral value', *Higher Education Research and Development*, 37(6), 1124–1140. doi: 10.1080/07294360.2018.1479378

Clarkson, P., and Gilbert, M. (1991) 'The training of counsellor trainers and supervisors'. In Dryden W., and Thorne, B. (Eds.), *Training and supervision for counselling in action* (pp. 143–169). London, England: Sage.

Cotterall, S. (2013) 'More than just a brain: Emotions and the doctoral experience,' *Higher Education Research & Development*, 32(2), 174–187.

Covey, S. (1989) *The seven habits of highly effective people*. New York: Simon and Schuster.

Elliot, D. L., Bengsten, S. S. E., Guccione, K., and Kobayashi, S. (2020) *The hidden curriculum in doctoral education*. London: Palgrave Macmillan. ISBN 9783030414962. doi: 10.1007/978-3-030-41497-9

Hughes, C., and Tight, M. (2013) 'The metaphors we study by: The doctorate as a journey and/or as work,' *Higher Education Research & Development*, 32(5), 765–775. doi: 10.1080/07294360.2013.777031

3 Developing your identity

By the end of this chapter you will

- Be able to consider the different aspects of your doctoral identity and how these connect.
- Develop a clearer understanding of the values of a part-time researcher identity and how to harness its benefits for the doctorate and within your professional life.
- Have identified aspects of your identity you might want to further develop and explore.

What's in store

Often, being part time can be seen as a disadvantage. This chapter aims to help you to explore the ways in which a part-time doctoral researcher identity can be a valuable asset for both your doctorate and your professional life. It aims to help you think more deeply about the competing aspects of your identity and how these might blend together to create a unique perspective. A series of activities will help you work through these aspects to consider your changing identity in a way that can benefit you. For different readers, there may

DOI : 10.4324/9781003223931-4

be different degrees or proportions of the "professional" aspect of your identity but as this chapter will show, you can still usefully consider the potential for clashes, using the idea of "competing identities."

What do we mean by identity?

Academic identity can be seen as something that changes over time but also represents how we make sense of ourselves (McAlpine et al., 2014). It has been framed as something shaped by institutions and disciplines but may also be shaped by professional networks (Drennen et al., 2020). For part-time doctoral researchers, things are more complex as there can be a blurring between academic and professional roles and identities. Equally, these identities might be compartmentalised and distinct, which can lead to a sense of not quite feeling like you fully fit in either. It is also important to acknowledge that identity formation is considered a social process and can be reinforced by connections to others within your institution and academic disciplines (Ching, 2021). However, for many part-time doctoral researchers, the opportunities for socialisation with others within the institution and within the wider academic field can be more limited than for full-time doctoral researchers. Chapter 7 helps you think about ways to build these connections through the notion of a support village.

Real-world reflection – juggling a professional and doctoral identity

Dr Sharon Inglis completed her Doctorate in Education in 2020 at Staffordshire University that examined the expectations and experiences of part-time students in transition into taught postgraduate students, and the staff who taught them. You can connect with her on Twitter @sharoninglis. She has reflected on the challenges of balancing a professional and researcher identity:

> It can be challenging to be a doctoral student in the institution where you work. Total immersion in your studies is a given, but it can be something of a double-edged sword.
>
> **Advantages**
> - Staying focused really isn't a problem, because your topic is all you ever think about and (almost) all you ever do.
> - You are most certainly immersed in your data because you have lived and breathed it.
> - Your recommendations write themselves. Your data screams at you! You know what needs to be done, and by the time that you have submitted, you're already halfway to evaluating your first attempt at implementation.
>
> **Disadvantages**
> - Total immersion means that there is no escape from either your doctorate or the day job.
> - Because your research and your day job are closely intertwined, it can be difficult for colleagues and management to be as sympathetic to your research as they would be if you were doing something completely different.

- If you are researching your own institution's students, you need to be particularly careful about perceptions of power.
- If your participants are your own students, then there is an added layer of complexity about your dual role.

How to successfully manage a dual identity

1. Reflecting upon your positionality in your own institution is a valuable addition to your thesis. Just remember to capture what you did before you forget!
2. Ring-fence your time and set clear boundaries for colleagues and students.
3. Manage expectations. For students, book your leave and communicate it well ahead. For colleagues, and anyone else who might be emailing you, have a polite but firm out-of-office response for time that you have committed to writing. Provide alternative contact details for your non-contact time.
4. Remember that as a part-time student, you eat the elephant that is your doctorate one bite at a time. Think about what you can usefully do in a small chunk of time (even if that's not how you would normally work).
5. Keep your eyes on the prize. You are investigating your own practice because you are passionate. If you didn't care about it so much that it hurts, you wouldn't be doing this. Breathe deeply, stick with it.

Adapted from Sharon's original blog post: https://thrivingparttime.com/2021/03/01/own-institution-doctoral-research-evaluating-total-immersion/

Activity: How does this chapter relate to me

Before we begin to explore issues of identity, it is a good idea to map out what you already know. We will do this through a freewriting exercise. For each of the prompts, write for three minutes without editing, censoring yourself, or stopping. If you run out of things to write, simply write "I do not know what else to write" until another idea comes to you.

Why are you doing a doctorate and how does this relate to your professional identity?

How might your identity change during the doctorate?

Once you have completed this, go back through your freewrite and highlight any key words, ideas, or themes. This can be a useful point for thinking about what aspects of your identity are important to you and what concerns you might want to reflect upon in this chapter.

Being part time

There are many reasons for undertaking a part-time doctorate. As highlighted in Chapter 1, many part-time doctorates are vocational so it is likely some of this chapter may feel less relevant if you are undertaking a part-time doctorate primarily to develop your knowledge of a topic for personal development. We would argue, however, that developing an identity in relation to your research is important. Doing a doctorate is in many ways unlike being a student on a taught qualification. You are becoming an expert in your subject, and part of that process of becoming means developing your identity as such. Therefore, when we talk about splits in identity, that can be a split with your previous student identity, with your identity in your personal life, or indeed your past sense of self. As with all of the book, come to the activities with an open mind and take what is useful to you and park the rest. You may even find over the course of your doctorate that your focus and your future goals change, necessitating revisiting your identity.

There are many benefits of being part time such as increased time to account for parts of the process out of your control, thinking time, and the ability to continue to pursue personal and career goals alongside your doctorate. One of the real challenges, however, can be the split in your identity. This may make you feel like you are never fully in one place. A concept often used to think about this liminal space of not fitting in is that of being in the borderlands. This idea comes from the work of Anzaldúa (2012 [1987]), who frames the borderlands as a physical or metaphorical space where two or more cultures come together. Whilst she was talking about her experiences of a "cultural borderlands" between her Mexican and Anglo cultures, this concept can be applied to other cultural boundaries. Researchers such as Tutkal et al. (2021) looking at interdisciplinary PhDs have already drawn upon this concept. However, we think this concept is ideal for thinking through the positionality of the part-time doctoral researcher. The confluence of work, academic, and personal identities can create a clear borderland that can, in some ways, feel unsettling. Part-time researchers often also experience exclusions like those described by Tuktal et al. (2021: 332) such as "lack of recognition and legitimacy of the margins we inhabit." These concerns about ability to fit in are shared despite the very different contexts and rationales. Tutkal et al. (2021) also foreground the impact being unfunded can have on the sense of belonging, an issue that often also plagues part-time doctoral researchers and makes this a really useful concept to use.

However, it is important to remember that inhabiting the borderlands is not always a bad thing. In fact, existing between spaces can give you unique and valuable insights to take into both worlds – the professional and the academic. As Anzaldúa (2012 [1987]) highlights, inhabitants of borderlands can have unique perspectives. Understanding this and embracing it can be useful in the development of your identity. Taking control of these borderlands can help you form your own identity that integrates aspects of the separate selves. To do this, you need to first explore how you got into these borderlands. There can be several reasons why you embarked on a part-time doctorate but often these will fall into one of two camps: design or necessity. Some of you may have a foot in both camps but understanding why you are here is often key to helping make sense of your identity.

You could also think about your time in the borderlands as a key part of your journey. It is important not to just rush through to an unknown destination as there is as much value in the journey as where you are going. It is this moving from one space to another that is likely to allow you to bring insights to your research that are unique to you and your experiences.

By design

For many of you, you may have an established career you love. Your doctorate is a complement to that. It might be directly related to your professional practice, tangential or a completely unrelated passion project. Your journey onto the part-time doctorate could be a continuation of a well-established history of part-time study or it might be your first time juggling the student and worker identity. Either way, you have consciously chosen to be here. You have seen the merits of part-time study and it works for you.

Being here by design, however, does not always mean things are plain sailing. Even those who deliberately choose to work in this way may have times where there are conflicts between their identities. You may also find that over the length of the doctorate that demands on your energies shift and this transforms what was initially a good fit of identities into identities that then exist in tension with each other. For example, changing jobs may either bring the research closer to your work life, or further away. Both can have implications for your doctoral journey so are worth considering early on.

By necessity

For some of you, the intention might have been to undertake the doctorate full time, but there were barriers to releasing this ambition. Perhaps funding wasn't available or forthcoming, or you simply could not afford to live on a stipend. It is also important to acknowledge that health and disability are valid reasons as to why part time might be the only viable option. If you are here by necessity, you may also have started full time but for various reasons needed to reduce the study intensity to allow more space for other demands on your life. It may also be that in some ways doing a doctorate was never purely a choice of your own making. It might have been a stipulation to continue working in your field and you see it primarily as a necessary hoop to jump through. In any of these cases, part time may have been less of a preferred choice, and more the only choice.

The reason for highlighting this divide between choice and necessity is that in many ways this might be a factor in maintaining your motivation. If we are doing something because we have to, or primarily for an external reason, it is often harder to keep going. It is therefore important to look beyond the necessity; you need to want to succeed, otherwise something else will always be more important. Even if you are here not entirely by choice, it is important to focus on the positives the part-time mode can bring and to identify the reasons why it works for you. It may also be that you have to move from full time to part time during the course of your doctorate. This can feel like a negative but actually, as we hope this book highlights, the part-time route can provide many benefits. Embracing and owning being part time as a badge of honour and not something to hide can often be key to integrating the identity of part-time doctoral researcher into your life. This can be especially important for those who hold what Billot et al. (2021) call dual-status academic lives – those working in higher education whilst also undertaking a doctorate – as it can help those two conflicting identities to be integrated, echoing some of the issues Sharon touched upon in her real-world example.

Internal and external identities

There are likely to be tensions between how you perceive yourself (your internal identity) and how others see you (your external identity). This is also likely to shift from one context to another. As you become more embedded within your research, you may feel like your perspectives are changing or indeed you might be starting to question some of the assumptions of your professional world whilst simultaneously still having to exist within that world.

Whilst on the surface others may see you as the same person, your sense of self may be changing.

For many of those around you, their understandings of your identity are based on their past knowledge and as you grow and develop. There may also be both positive and negative preconceptions people make when they know you are undertaking a doctorate. Furthermore, our identity is also likely to change over the course of the doctorate. The experience is not only about knowledge but is one that is in many ways transformative. Therefore, it is important to be aware that this can create tensions. This split in identities, or as Bourdieu might describe it a cleft habitus (Friedman, 2015), can lead to feeling like you both fit in and feel out of place in multiple spaces. For example, you might feel like you are becoming distanced from your professional context whilst not feeling like you fit in in the world of academia. However, Abrahams and Ingram's (2013) notion that we can be chameleon-like is helpful here as we can and do have the ability to shift and adapt into new environments, even when they might feel quite alien. In contrast, whilst the split between identities is often framed negatively, there can also be many positives from juggling multiple identities and the insights this places you in the unique position to see.

Juggling demands on your time

This theme of competing demands runs through the book. In fact, in thinking about your map in the last chapter, you probably have already begun to reflect upon these. Other than the need to decide how to balance competing demands, one of the most daunting aspects of the part-time doctorate is the sheer number of things you need to juggle over an extended period. Most full-time students will have to maintain this balance for far shorter periods and will often have less breadth of things to juggle. They are also more likely to involve very diverse tasks, some of which might be less under your control than if you were focusing on your own research as your main priority. Chapter 5 will examine how to manage competing tasks. However, it is not just tasks that need juggling. You are probably going to be juggling identities. These often include employee (or employer), parent, partner, friend, student, academic, teacher, mentor, etc. Understanding why these competing identities are important to you is an important step in considering how to prioritise the more practical elements.

Real-world reflection – when work and research are worlds apart

Dawn Weeden is currently undertaking a part-time PhD in Musicology at The Open University whilst continuing to work as a full-time accountant. She reflects on how this actually can work well:

> For the last 40 years my professional life has revolved around accountancy and tax, working as a practitioner as well as a lecturer and examiner. I currently work full time as an in-house accountant for a group of companies. In October 2021 I embarked on a part-time PhD researching Salvation Army Brass Band Music.
>
> There are inevitable tensions between my identities as a professional accountant (an economic necessity) and a researcher (the fascinating

and fun element), but there are also benefits to being involved in two contrasting disciplines. Skills honed in my professional life – analysing data, explaining concepts, written and verbal presentations – are equally essential to my role as a researcher. Motivation to study and enthusiasm for my research topic is maintained by the enforced break that the day job necessitates. Additionally, and perhaps most importantly, working on mundane accountancy tasks allows research ideas to percolate subconsciously – I always carry a research notebook so that I can capture thoughts as they occur.

The primary challenge for me is time management, and the accompanying guilt when I have to prioritise work over research. There are statutory deadlines in accountancy that dictate my work patterns, and this impacts on the hours I have available for research. I quickly discovered that setting aside 20 hours every week to devote to my studies was impossible. My solution is to plan out available time on an annual basis: First plotting in the accountancy deadlines and then blocking out research time. I am also fortunate in having an employer who, while not really understanding why I want to spend six years undertaking a PhD "for fun" is supportive, and allows me flexibility to change my working hours to fit around training, supervision sessions, and research days.

To anyone considering or undertaking a doctorate in a different field to your paid employment I would recommend embracing the crossover of skills between employment and research.

Getting your employer on board can help but you also need to accept that there will be times when work takes priority over research.

Activity: What are your identities?

Now would be a good time to stop and take stock of the identities you juggle (or might anticipate juggling if you are just starting out). You might feel at this stage that there is no connection between them, but come to this activity with an open mind and you might find connections you did not realise existed.

Take a sheet of paper and set your timer for two minutes. Try not to overthink this task, just jot down every identity that comes to mind. There is no need for full sentences; use single words and phrases and dot them around the page.

For example, these might include student, parent, boss, carer, runner, etc.

What connections can you make between these?

What identities feel most comfortable to you at the moment?

How might you be able to become more comfortable in the other identities you have listed?

Make a few brief notes on your initial thoughts here. You might want to revisit these as the doctorate progresses or as you situation changes over time.

Becoming a researcher

When we decide to embark on doctoral study, we take on a whole wealth of new identities to go alongside our existing ones. Unlike a full-time researcher, you are often going to be adding new identities rather than replacing existing ones. Therefore, for part-time researchers this can also add a level of complexity. Drawing back on Anzaldúa (2012 [1987]:25) and the notion of borderlands, this identity is often in a "constant state of transition." Researchers have written about the role of multiple identities (e.g., Barnacle and Mewburn, 2010) but some of the most relevant work here comes from Lynn McAlpine (2012) on how your identity as a doctoral researcher is shaped by who you are, where you come from, your current circumstances, and imagined futures. In Chapter 2, we took you through the idea of drawing a metaphorical map and considering these aspects. We also got you to think about what your imagined futures would look like. Building upon that, we are now going to consider how you can take those initial ideas through into developing your own researcher identity.

One of the keys to developing your identity is to develop an understanding of what McAlpine (2012) calls "opportunity structures." These can be thought of as the possible pathways following your doctorate. For many of you, this might be staying primarily within your current roles, it might involve developing a "side-hustle" such as writing or consultancy work, or indeed it might be about moving to a new career based on your research either inside or outside of academia. All of these pathways are valid but the way you might want to develop your identity to support you in these desired trajectories can vary. What is key to ensure that you are prepared for this transition is to reflect upon this, asking yourself what possible avenues you might want to explore. We deliberately use the plural here as keeping a broad mind often helps if life changes, the labour market changes, or your personal goals change over time.

Researcher-practitioner-something else?

For many of you reading this book, developing a researcher identity is only part of the story. The activities may have highlighted to you that you are already faced with tensions between several competing identities, and this is normal. If you are completing a practice-based doctorate, it might be that your artist identity is central to who you are. Likewise, for those doing a professional doctorate, being an educator, a healthcare practitioner, an entrepreneur, or whatever your area of expertise is might be more central to your core identity than that of a researcher.

In fact, tacit knowledge from practice can be extremely valuable in some areas. In many cases your research probably could not be done by someone who does not have your professional expertise. The bad news, though, is that often this valuable expertise is undervalued in the structures and systems of academia. As we have mentioned previously, there is a "hidden" language underpinning higher education that, when you are not familiar with it, can cause you to feel inadequate however experienced you are in other aspects of your life or career. This can lead to a sense of imposter syndrome or what we hear doctoral researchers describe as "not feeling academic enough." Part of the doctoral process is about learning how to frame things within academic conventions, so it is normal to feel like this, but it is also important to talk these issues through with peers and perhaps your supervisors.

A lot of your identity is also likely to be related to your motivations for doing a doctorate. For many of you, we expect it is likely to stem from a desire to know more about your field or area of interest. For others, however, it might be a requisite for your employment. Acknowledging this is important to help you understand how to integrate these identities, as even if you are embarking on this journey as a necessity to career progression, it is still likely to impact upon your sense of identity to some extent.

It is also important to note that just because you are doing a professional doctorate, it does not mean it will have an impact on your professional practice unless there is a conscious effort to ensure overlap between your professional and doctoral worlds (Creaton, 2021). Within Creaton's interviews with those doing professional doctorates, some participants were surprised that the end of the thesis process was often the end of their relationship with the university. If being a researcher or academic is part of the identity you want to inhabit after completion, this is something that you need to develop and might want to reflect more on when we move to chapter 7 on building your village.

Researching in the workplace?

As was highlighted in Sharon Inglis' real-world reflection, part-time doctoral researchers often experience tensions between their paid employment and their doctorate. This is most acute when you are either researching directly in the workplace or researching an area close to practice. Billot et al. (2021) highlights the often-held tensions between being a competent professional and a novice researcher. This applies in any number of professional contexts, often most acutely for staff in higher education who are also doctoral researchers. One of the things to be aware of when inhabiting this borderland of research in the workplace is the possibility for destabilisation of your identity. It is easy to let feelings of inexperience as a researcher challenge your more established identity as a professional, which can result in crises of confidence.

Supporting identity development

One of the key ways you are supported in becoming an academic researcher is through the supervisory relationship, which is dealt with in more depth in Chapter 4. Really, though, this is only one part of the puzzle. Certainly, supervisors can be excellent at supporting your intellectual and skill development; however, your identity as a doctoral researcher is likely to be more complex. You will be finding your feet within an environment that is often very different to that which your supervisor developed theirs in. Many supervisors will have been full-time doctoral researchers and so often their lived experience may be different. Likewise, they will have entered job markets at a different time or often had different imagined futures. This is where developing other forms of support can be valuable.

Networking can play a key role in helping you develop your identity. There are two ways of thinking about this. One is the more obvious, interpersonal networking that we will discuss in Chapter 7. Slightly less obvious is McAlpine's (2012) notion of intertextual networking. This is how reading and engaging with literature can create networks of scholars with similar concerns and thinking. We would also argue that there is another point between the two, the role of interpersonal networking in written online forms.

Being an academic is far broader than your thesis or even your research. In fact, there are aspects of your identity you may feel you need to develop that are not immediately catered for within your doctoral program or through wider networking. This means you may need to seek out opportunities to develop these, which can be achieved through seeking out voluntary roles or professional development opportunities. For example, you might gain experience in budgeting and event management by volunteering to help with event organisation. There may also be opportunities for being a representative on a committee in a sector body or in your institution. Both offer a chance to gain experience and wider academic skills. Similarly, taking up opportunities to review papers for conferences or academic journals enables you to develop a wider understanding of the review process and a chance to work with other academics. Even if you cannot commit the time to do some of these activities, there may be workshops on funding, peer review, and data management that can help you gain a better understanding of these aspects of academic work.

Towards a hybrid identity

As this chapter has shown, the identities of a part-time doctoral student can be complex. We are sure many of you reading this already knew that. Trying to fit into one box, however, can be the biggest challenge. In thinking about pathways outside of academia following the doctorate, Skakni (2021) has proposed the value of developing a hybrid identity which values your unique skills and experiences. This also resonates with our thinking in this chapter about your identity as a part-time doctoral researcher. As part-time doctoral researchers, you possess a nexus of talents, skills, and insights that is invaluable and should be embraced and celebrated as a unique identity as opposed to attempting to adapt it to fit within existing boxes.

We cannot promise this will always be a comfortable experience. Thinking back to Anzaldúa's (2012 [1987]) ideas of borderlands and identity, she writes:

> knowledge makes me more aware; it makes me more conscious. "Knowing" is painful because after it happens, I can't stay in the same place and be comfortable. I am no longer the same person I was before.
>
> (70)

This, for those researching areas close to practice, can be an unsettling process. However, it can also be liberating. What it may entail though is going back to Chapter 2 and rethinking your map because what you thought were your long-term goals may change significantly during this process of discovering your identity.

What is important to remember when the doubts creep in about being not good enough or out of place is that you have successfully got this far. You have succeeded in your previous academic studies, and you have been accepted onto a doctoral program. Working out how to make this work for you is, of course, a challenge, but if other people did not believe in you, you would not be reading this right now. Remember one of the key criteria of a doctorate is a contribution to knowledge and often this is driven by your own experience and perspectives, ones made richer by having a hybrid identity.

What you have discovered in this chapter would make a useful addition to your "route map" created in Chapter 2. We suggest that you revisit your map and continue to annotate it, based on your learning in this chapter.

Researchers recommend ...

- Being a part-time doctoral researcher can mean wearing more than one hat and having more than one identity. This shouldn't be something to shy away from but to own and embrace.
- You are unique in the identities and positions you inhabit. This can give you a unique perspective on the world and on your research.
- Identities can and do change over time. Although this might create some discomfort, understanding what is important to you can help you reconcile them.

Where can I find out more?

For consideration of your professional identity and presentation on social media, we highly recommend Mark Carrigan's (2020) *Social Media for Academics*.

References

Abrahams, J., & Ingram, N. (2013) 'The chameleon habitus: Exploring local students' negotiations of multiple fields', *Sociological Research Online*, 18(4), 21. Retrieved from http://www.socresonline.org.uk/18/4/21.html

Anzaldúa, G. (2012 [1987]) *Borderlands/La Frontera- the new Mestiza*. San Francisco: Aunt Lute Books.

Barnacle, R., & Mewburn, I. (2010) 'Learning networks and the journey of "becoming doctor"', *Studies in Higher Education*, 35(4), 433–444. doi:10.1080/03075070903131214

Billot, J., King, V., Smith, J., & Clouder, L. (2021) 'Borderlanders: Academic staff being and becoming doctoral students', *Teaching in Higher Education*, 26(3), 438–453. doi:10.1080/13562517.2021.1891408

Carrigan, M. (2020) *Social media for academics* (2nd edition). London: Sage.

Ching, G. S. (2021) 'Academic identity and communities of practice: Narratives of social science academics career decisions in Taiwan', *Education Sciences*, 11(8), 388.

Creaton, J. (2021) 'The impact of professional doctorates in the workplace: Evidence from the criminal justice sector', *Research in Post-Compulsory Education*, 26(3), 274–289. doi: 10.1080/13596748. 2021.1920259

Drennan, J., Clarke, M., Hyde, A. and Politis, Y., (2020) 'Academic identity in higher education', In Teixeira, P. and Shin, J.C. (eds.). *The international encyclopaedia of higher education systems and institutions*. Dordrecht: Springer Netherlands, pp.35–40.

Friedman, S. (2015) 'What is the habitus clivé?', *The Sociological Review Magazine*. https://thesociologicalreview.org/collections/interviews/what-is-the-habitus-cliv%C3%A9/ (Accessed 11th April 2022).

McAlpine, L. (2012) 'Identity-trajectories: Doctoral journeys from past to present to future', *The Australian Universities' Review*, 54(1), 38–46. https://search.informit.org/doi/10.3316/ielapa.424355529639257

McAlpine, L., Amundsen, C. and Turner, G. (2014) 'Identity-trajectory: Reframing early career academic experience', *British Educational Research Journal*, 40(6), 952–969. doi: 10.1002/berj.3123

Skakni, I. (2021) 'Taking your researcher identity outside the university's walls', *The hidden curriculum in doctoral education*. Available at: https://drhiddencurriculum.wordpress.com/2021/06/15/taking-your-researcher-identity-outside-the-universitys-walls/ (Accessed 11 April 2022).

Tutkal, S., Busnelli, V., Castelao-Huerta, I., Barbosa dos Santos, F., Loaiza Orozco, L. F., & Rivera Arcila, D. (2021) 'Inhabiting borders: Autoethnographic reflections of PhD students in Colombia', *Teaching in Higher Education*, 26(3), 321–339. doi: 10.1080/13562517.2021.1895108

4 Working with your supervisor(s)

By the end of this chapter, you will have

- Considered some of the tensions, possibilities, benefits, and challenges of supervision partnerships.
- Developed a clearer understanding of the many roles a supervisor may take and considered how these fit with the support you require through your doctorate.
- Thought about what you can do to ensure you get off to a good start with your supervisor(s).
- Identified priority topics to further explore in conversation with your supervisor(s).

What's in store

Negotiating and sustaining a good working partnership with your supervisor or supervisory team is a shared endeavour and requires conscious effort and dedicated time. In this chapter we draw upon opinions from both part-time researchers and the supervisors of part-time researchers to offer you a comparison of expectations

DOI : 10.4324/9781003223931-5

and perspectives that we hope you will find enlightening as you consider your own supervision needs. Through a series of guided activities, we will support you to define a realistic supervision wish list, and to communicate with your supervisor(s) in a way that will benefit you.

What does a supervisor do?

Many of us on beginning our doctorates know we will work with a supervisor or supervisory team, but we do not know what to expect from those supervisors. We understand that supervision is intended to be a helping relationship, a guiding relationship, and will give us access to a more senior researcher with specialist expertise in our chosen area of study. But what will they specifically offer you? What roles can a supervisor take? What kind of interactions will take place? How will the team work together to support you? What are their responsibilities, and what are yours? In recent years we have seen the production of guidance at the national level in the UK context from organisations such as the UK Council for Graduate Education who produced the first national Good Supervisory Practice Framework (UKCGE, 2019), which acknowledges the wide-ranging, highly complex, and demanding set of roles involved in modern research supervision and encourages supervisors to develop supervision as a conscious professional practice. The Australian Council of Graduate Research also recognises the critical role of supervisors via their Good Practice Guidelines for Quality Graduate Research Supervision (ACGR, 2021) which make recommendations to universities for how they should support and develop supervisors to ensure the highest quality of supervision. One recommendation the ACGR guidance makes is that individual universities should each set out good principles in relation to best practice in supervision in alignment with the context for their institution. When each of us is, therefore, forming our own expectations for supervision, we may find assistance in these kinds of university documents. These can be known locally as codes of practice for doctoral degrees, a doctorate programme handbook, or even as a standalone statement of expectations for good supervision, produced by your university, in line with their ambitions to create positive and supportive cultures. These documents, whilst providing an overview, can be hugely variable in the level of detail and specificity they contain, making them more or less useful to individual postgraduate researchers and supervisors who are trying to understand what good practice in supervision means and how to interact with each other.

In the absence of clear guidance we can tend to make assumptions about what a supervisor is, and what they do. We all enter new projects, roles, and working partnerships with expectations about how things will go. We draw upon our previous educational experiences to form these expectations and that can mean that we make assumptions about what it will be like to work with a supervisor, what their role is or how they will expect us to interact with them. Part-time doctoral researchers often tend to have prior experience of a range of professional relationships too, and so expectations of supervision as a professional guiding role can be based on what is already known and experienced in previous professional contexts. You may yourself recognise that you are holding some assumptions about your supervisor and what you can expect them to provide. Consider how you react to these statements concerning the role of a supervisor. A supervisor is

- A more knowledgeable researcher.
- A source of motivation and enthusiasm.
- The arbiter of your future career.
- A tour guide who will keep you on track.
- The boss, to be obeyed.
- Someone whose role focuses entirely on supporting postgraduate researchers.
- The person who leads the research project you will complete.
- Someone you need to impress at all times.
- A resource you can access as needed.
- A line manager who is familiar with organisational policies and processes.
- Someone you can confide in and trust with personal information.
- A "guardian of the discipline" who maintains the academic standards required.

Are any of the preceding statements true? The answer is not a universal yes or a universal no. You might find some to be common sense and others to be clearly inappropriate. Which is which will vary from person to person. All those statements are true in some supervisory partnerships, in some circumstances, and as the situation requires. There will be other roles a supervisor takes too, in addition to the selection listed here. What supervision looks like for one researcher may be quite different from that of another, depending on your project, circumstances, experience, and preferences. Similarly, the kind of support a supervisor provides will naturally change over time as you progress, and as you face new situations and challenges along the way. The dynamic nature of the partnership means that what is important is the quality of the communication between you, and your openness to discussing the dynamics of supervision and how things are going. Awareness, understanding, and empathy is key to building an effective partnership, and our aim for this chapter is to guide you in creating these elements.

A co-constructed partnership

As a part-time doctoral researcher you may already know your supervisor(s) relatively well, or you may be meeting and getting to know them for the first time through your course. You may be a regular face in the department, or you may be studying at a distance and meeting via an online platform. Additionally, you may be looking for advice on recruiting a new supervisor to your team mid-degree as happens commonly, for example in situations where the need for specialist expertise arises, or if one of your team takes an extended period of leave, retires, or moves institutions. This chapter has been designed to support you to be aware of your options and to consider your strengths and needs whatever your current circumstances, because knowing these are the basis of making good supervision choices.

From the perspective of taught or professional doctorates, a part-time doctorate may provide a year or more as part of a cohort that proves a research community guided by a heterogenous group of academic staff with different styles, experiences, and specialisms. This is a great opportunity to get to know the people who are likely to supervise you at the later stages of the programme. Noticing individual supervisors' tendencies towards the roles listed earlier, and indeed asking them directly about their views on the role of a supervisor and communicating how you like to work can help you to enter the research phase feeling more informed about what to expect. Similarly, you may have completed a master's degree with the same supervisor, or perhaps worked alongside them as an academic colleague. This is also helpful in shaping your expectations for how to work together. Notably though, there will be work to do together for all these scenarios. Even if you know each other well, there will be a shift in the roles you occupy at the point you begin a supervisory partnership. This may be visible as a change in your relative status, a change in the power balance, the institutional expectations for your degree, or in terms of how you relate to each other. It may be that you have come into this chapter looking for ways to make changes for the positive, and all the ideas we offer can support that too. In summary, it is worth your time to pay attention to the (re)setting of expectations, even if you already know your supervisor(s).

If you browse the literature on doctoral supervision, you may notice the tendency of the sector to talk of supervision as something that can "make or break" a student (Lee, 2008). This is because the research studies available, as well as the experiences of those of us who work as professionals in postgraduate researcher development and supervisor development roles, highlight the influence of good supervision on sustained motivation, timely completion, and landmarks of academic success such as publication and career progression. A 2018 study by Bryan and Guccione found that the supervisory experience was one of the major factors in whether graduates judged their doctorate to have been worth the time and energy they put into it. It would be remiss of us not to emphasise the crucial role of supervision in how you will experience your doctorate. It is a close working relationship that has to be sustained over many years, often six or seven years, part time. In addition, part-time researchers, especially those who are not regularly physically present in their department, can be less likely to have easy access to a group of peers, which can increase your feelings of being isolated or distant from the research community and increase your reliance on direct contact with the supervisory team to provide you with reassurance, guidance, and support. Indeed, a reflection by Rainford (2020) argues that a supervisor of part-time postgraduates should specifically seek to help them to make connections to the research community. Their position within the discipline, as both a gatekeeper and a facilitating link that can connect you to local and global research communities, increases the importance of cultivating a good supervision relationship.

The good news is that you can influence the quality of the supervision relationship. A good partnership is one that is openly discussed and is designed specifically for the way you both need to work, be that online, in person, at regular intervals, or designed to fit into small spaces of time in and around your work, life, and family commitments. Being open about what you need from your supervisor helps to build trust between you. Professional relationships always require active input to manage and maintain, and the supervision relationship is no different in that sense. The following activities and pointers will support you to do this well by guiding you to co-construct your supervisory partnership(s). As you progress through this chapter, we suggest that you might either involve your supervisor(s) directly in the activities and discuss the ideas together, or if it feels more appropriate to you, that you might indirectly feed the outcomes of your reflections into your regular supervision meetings and ongoing progress reviews.

Activity: What do you value in a professional relationship?

This activity asks you to reflect on a prior professional relationship that has worked well for you. It may help you – and your supervisor(s) if they are willing to take part – to reflect on what you consider to be the elements of a successful working relationship. It is informative to know what types of interaction help you to be at your best, and what past experiences may be unconsciously influencing your expectations for supervision.

Take a couple of minutes to think back to a learning relationship or other professional relationship that you found supportive and enabling. This may be with a teacher or tutor, with a peer, or with a manager or senior leader.

What types of communications, interactions, and scenarios did I respond positively to?
What did I react negatively to?
What did I respect about my colleague?
What did they respect about me?
What elements do I feel were key to the previous successful partnership?

Take a sheet of paper and set a timer for one minute for each of the preceding five questions. Try not to censor yourself; no one else will read these notes and what you produce doesn't have to be perfect. Work in sentences, words, phrases, or pictures as you prefer.

Thinking about these things can help you understand and articulate the elements of a supervision partnership that works for you. And remember that a good working partnership is about what you can give, as well as what you can get.

The preceding activity can help to ground your supervision relationships in your preferences for how you want to be treated as a person. First and foremost, you are a person, and part of that whole person is a researcher. In studies that ask supervisors what influences their approach to supervision, they note that their own formative supervision experiences combine with the institutional regulations and support, the conventions of the discipline, and cultural and personal preferences of the individual postgraduate researcher (Whittington et al., 2021). Part-time doctoral researchers are complex people; you will have a tendency to have rich and demanding home and working lives and be influenced by multiple identities and responsibilities, as we discussed previously in Chapter 3. The influential nature of these identities, experiences, positions, and preferences should not be overlooked in favour of focusing solely on your academic development needs. Note too, that supervisors are also real people with preferences, values, organisational constraints, and different competing priorities. This is why we suggested previously, and ahead, that you involve your supervisor(s) directly in discussion of the ideas this chapter presents. As Dr Louise Harris's following vignette demonstrates, supervisors who are skilled and experienced in supervising part-time researchers are able to offer academic support tailored to each student within the context of their personal circumstances. Good communication on both sides is required.

Real-world reflection – adapting to each researcher

Dr Louise Harris, Senior Lecturer in Sonic and Audiovisual Practices at the University of Glasgow discusses her approach:

The overriding thing that guides my own practice is the acknowledgment that when it comes to approaching, developing, and defining the supervisory relationship, one size definitely doesn't fit all. There are so many reasons why this is the case – just as there are so many reasons why doctoral students choose to study part time – and accounting for each individual's circumstance and their associated needs is key to developing an effective, productive, and equitable supervisory relationship. For example, part-time students may be balancing parenting or caring responsibilities, they may be established professionals approaching their doctorate as a way of consolidating their practice, they may be self-funding and working long hours to support their studies. Equally, some students prefer to study part-time just to give the research process longer to breathe and develop – in my experience, I have found this to be particularly true for practice-based researchers. Studying part time means that each student will have their own pattern of work and way of approaching their research – there may be periods of time where they're able to devote a lot of attention to their doctoral studies and require a sudden flurry of supervisory input; equally, there may be other periods where they don't manage to devote so much time to developing their work. Each student therefore requires an individual approach to the supervisory relationship – some respond to regularity of meetings, setting of deadlines, checking in on progress; others prefer to be left alone until they feel ready to report for input and discussion. Adapting and responding to each doctoral student and what they need is really important – just as it's important to make sure you create an open, honest, and respectful relationship with them where they feel able to tell you what they need to make things work. This can also help them to develop confidence in their work and their expertise; ultimately, they'll become the authority on the thing they're researching, and encouraging them to embrace that whilst giving ourselves the opportunity to reflect on what we can learn through supervising their project can be both very productive and very rewarding.

The preceding account, making a case for communication that enables openness, empathy, and flexibility, stands in stark contrast to the following one, from an anonymous part-time doctoral researcher.

Real-world reflection – clashing expectations for supervision

A researcher in data science shares their experience of feeling lost, both in their doctorate and in the parameters of their supervision relationship.

I went along to the bi-monthly meetings the dept regulations said we were supposed to have, but what was happening in supervision was I was just trying to guess what I was supposed to say and failing to know what support I was supposed to be receiving. It feels really daft now looking back because in my "real life" outside my PhD, I am a senior staff member in my profession. I'm used to moving projects forward. I just wasn't sure what I was supposed to ask for, or report on, as there was no organisational demand for the work to be done, and no deadline to deliver the various pieces, just me and my curiosity and no framework. The guidance we got at induction said we were to meet, but not what to discuss. I brought some outline plans in to the first couple of meetings, but my supervisor said she wanted to know what I had read in the literature. Well, I was planning to read what was needed if the plans were approved, so I had to say I'd read nothing. She was concerned that I hadn't "stepped into the role of a PhD student." This affected my whole PhD for months. I still don't know what it was that I didn't know back then, but I am finding my way through slowly, realising that it's up to me to be clear about what I want from my supervisor. I honestly felt there were some unspoken rules somewhere and I couldn't access them. Feeling so ignorant is paralysing, so I just shut down. I should have just said something to my supervisor and put a stop to the uncertainty, but I was too embarrassed, so I let it go on until I was really not enjoying my PhD at all.

A realistic grounding for supervisory support

Getting answers to your questions and requesting the academic support you need from your supervisor is not an easy thing to do, as we saw in the preceding vignette.

This is because you have (most likely) never completed a doctorate before and you don't know what the process requires of you or what you are likely to need. Additionally, it is likely that you have not been supervised at this level before and so the dynamics of the partnership are unfamiliar, making you unsure of the types of role(s) a supervisor will adopt in service of your academic training. Additionally, as a part-time researcher it's likely that you will be spending a considerable amount of time (if not all of your doctoral time) studying remotely from your department and supervisor, meeting online at scheduled points. As the more experienced party, and given the power asymmetry in the supervision relationship, perhaps the onus should be on the supervisor to reduce students' feelings of vulnerability (Jacobsen et al., 2021), but in reality they may not always have the awareness or context to anticipate what you need. You can help them understand what you need from them, but first it might be good to revisit the idea of expectations again and this time look at some common unrealistic supervisor expectations and supervisory myths that can derail the partnership. These themes have been collated from conversations with doctoral researchers who felt their expectations were not being met, and with some unpicking we can see how this has happened. While the following list would be useful to inform a supervisory conversation between all new doctoral researchers and their supervisors, openly addressing these myths can prove particularly informative to part-time supervisory partnerships in which the relationship is likely to take longer to build, with fewer opportunities for day-to-day interactions and observations of each other's preferences. Consider each in turn, and how this maps to your current understanding.

Myth: Your supervisor will have all the answers to your questions. In reality: There might not yet be answers to some of the questions you have. The doctorate is a process of original discovery and the creation of new knowledge, and there might not be an established "right way" or a defined pathway to follow. Similarly, your supervisor cannot be an expert in your career or in selecting the "right choice" for you. A good supervisor will be able to articulate what is known, what is a subjective opinion or a contested concept, and what they themselves do not yet know.

Myth: Your supervisor will be an exact disciplinary match. In reality: Most academics supervise across a variety of related research topics. While they can generally offer "big picture" expertise in the field and guidance in the process of producing original research, they can't be an expert in every detail, especially if you yourself have devised the project you are working on. The two of you together will combine your knowledge to create a way forward.

Myth: Your supervisor will have read every paper and book. In reality: With the best will in the world, no one of us can have read everything there is to read. You can ask for direct recommended starting points, and then follow your interests and bring your findings back to supervisions to share and talk through. Discussing your reading isn't a test of how well you have memorised your reading, it's an opportunity to make sense of the literature and how it applies to your research.

Myth: Your supervisor will tell you when it is time to write. In reality: Reading and writing are parallel processes that co-exist through the doctorate. A regular writing habit will help you to make sense of your reading, your methodology, your data analysis, and how these can all be meshed together to create the arguments you put forward in your thesis. In the absence of direct instruction to write specific things or at specific times, do it anyway. It can only help you both.

Myth: Your supervisor will be familiar with every university policy and procedure. In reality: Universities are vast organisations with many different processes and many different guiding policies governing every aspect of the doctoral experience, academic working life, and our legal, moral, and contractual obligations. These change frequently and can be difficult to keep abreast of until needed. All policies should be available to you as a member of your university, and if you are struggling to find the documents you need, ask your fellow researchers, your graduate school, or departmental PGR administrators for help.

Myth: Your supervisor will know everyone in your field. In reality: A supervisor who introduces you to others in the department and the discipline is invaluable. Your supervisors are likely to have had the opportunity to meet and work with more people than you have, but building large disciplinary networks is a process that takes time, funding, energy, and skill. It is absolutely fine if people haven't "heard of" your supervisor. It's to your benefit to build connections yourself, to make links through your peers, professional scholarly memberships, and even social media.

Myth: Your supervisor will be able to influence people on your behalf. In reality: All of us in university life are sometimes bound by rigid processes and constrained by what is possible within the context of the organisational rules and the national policies, legal obligations, sector regulations, and funding terms and conditions we come across. A good supervisor will support you to anticipate and navigate any obstacles that arise. They will be an advocate for you and will take action to ensure you are treated fairly and can access opportunities within the constraints that present themselves.

Myth: Your supervisor will only support you if you want to have an academic career. In reality: This kind of attitude is becoming increasingly rare, as a decreasing proportion of doctoral graduates stay in academia long term. Individual career aspirations and motivations for gaining a doctorate are personal to each individual and can change with experience of academic work. Part-time doctoral researchers may enter into a doctorate for professional development reasons, as a career change, to solve a professional problem through research, or as a personal challenge, and good supervisors can support you to seek both career guidance and opportunities that fit with your own motivations for "what's next."

We have covered some of the expectations of supervisors that new doctoral researchers can hold onto starting out, and a few of the myths that commonly cause a sense of dissatisfaction if they are borne of assumptions about what a supervisor will or can do. We have also offered you the opportunity to reflect on what you value in a professional relationship, which helps you to articulate your personal style, needs, and constraints and will inform how you and your supervisor communicate. The following activity is designed to help focus this into a loose template for what you might actually cover at each supervision meeting. A supervisor can adopt a role of "reducer of uncertainty" (Albertyn and Bennett, 2021), if you help them to understand what you are feeling uncertain about. At the same time, your supervisor, if not kept up to date, can begin to feel uncertain and worried about how things are going for you, whether you are making progress, and if you are feeling supported. You can help to reduce uncertainty for them by volunteering this information on a regular basis and keeping them in the loop with progress.

As part-time researchers are less likely to have a permanent workspace in the same physical space as their supervisor(s), a regular well-structured meeting and a defined follow-up process can make sure that you are communicating well. This is especially important for busy part-time researchers, as the time interval between supervisory meetings will tend to be longer than for full-time researchers and there may be a lot to cover at each supervision. You will want to make sure the meeting gets you what you need, as it can feel difficult to ask for more time when "popping in" to your supervisor's office isn't an option. Additionally, supervision via online platforms can be harder work, and you can encourage trust to develop between you if you take a structured approach and overtly make time to discuss topics such as personal life, career progression, and professional development, as well as academic progress. Further, regular updates on progress will ensure sure that you stay on your supervisor's "radar," that is, that your research and progress is regularly in their thoughts, and that they can make connections between you and your work, passing on ideas, opportunities, and information that may benefit you.

Activity: Setting the agenda for supervision meetings

This activity provides you with an outline of what you might cover in regular meetings with your supervisor(s) and is intended to be used, adapted, and updated throughout your doctorate in collaboration with your supervisor(s). Before a supervision meeting it will be helpful to think through the following points to prepare your mind, and even to prepare and circulate an agenda and notes ahead of the meeting.

What have I achieved since we last met? Include new learning, ideation, and reflection on reading or data, and new contacts made, as well as tangible written pieces, data gathered, or other academic products or outputs.

Is anything preventing me from making the progress I set out to make? Was it a reasonable amount of work to complete within the time frame? What got in the way? And what has been conducive to making good progress?

Professional development identified. What development in knowledge or skills will I access through my university, professional networks, or research community that helps me to overcome those barriers? Invite feedback from your supervisors to support your continued development.

How is my career developing through the doctorate? How have you developed a researcher or academic identity in recent weeks? How will this be useful beyond the doctorate? What different career paths are you considering post doctorate?

What progress do I intend to make by next time we meet? Be as specific as you can. Breaking larger tasks into smaller ones means that they are more likely to be achieved.

What would I like to learn from or discuss with my supervisor(s) that helps me to move forward with these plans? What feedback, resources, permissions, validation, or support do you need? What are your 'unknowns'?

After the meeting, send your supervisor(s) a summary of the above, including any points of difference or agreement, and specific actions you have agreed. This is very useful for checking everyone's understanding is the same, and also for documenting that you have made the agreed progress at the next meeting.

You can always follow up between meetings too, particularly if you are stuck, worried, or unable to make progress. Receiving early warning of difficulties on the horizon is always appreciated.

We hope your reading of this chapter has both made a case for open dialogue that rejects assumptions, and also offered you some ideas for how to manage the discussion and agreement of expectations, progress, and support from your supervisor(s). The final section of this chapter discusses how to engage with supervisory feedback.

Get the feedback you need

From the outset it is appropriate for your supervisor(s) to offer you some developmental feedback to support your learning and professional practice as a researcher. Getting supervisory feedback will not only help you design your study well, collect and analyse data appropriately, and communicate your own research findings clearly, but it will also help you to critically position the arguments in your thesis in accordance with the conventions of your discipline, ensuring impact and a developing reputation in your professional networks. Good supervisory teams will manage the feedback they give so that you receive one set of clear recommendations, and guidance for the future. If you find that this is not the case, and that you are receiving conflicting messages from the various members of your supervisory team, please know that you are not alone. In this case you could usefully add this topic to the next supervision meeting agenda and ask your primary supervisor for support in managing competing expectations. Periodically meeting all of your supervisors together as a panel can also help to reconcile opinions about the way forward for your doctorate. If your university doesn't require this as standard or have set dates for review with the whole supervisory team, you can make the suggestion and proactively manage the process of getting and agreeing their feedback.

From working for many years with doctoral learners, there are some important things about feedback we know. Even the most practised and proficient colleagues seem to have two modes of engaging in feedback that are hard to reconcile – perhaps you also find you have this tendency to inhabit both of the following roles? As the giving and receiving of feedback is a major way that trust can be built or broken with supervisors (Guccione, 2018), it is worth trying to bear in mind the following two perspectives:

- *As feedback giver*, more feedback equals more value. We come from a perspective of trying to offer as much input as possible to help the learner to develop. This means that we look closely for ways, big and small, in which we can help the learner improve. This may apply to a presentation or written work, or to offering general comments on project progress or career development. If we as the feedback giver can identify all the mistakes and offer a number of pointers or words of advice, we feel we have done a good job of supporting the learner.

- *As feedback recipient*, less is best. When we read a critique of our ideas, see a page full of "red pen" or track changes, or sit through a commentary of how we can do better or achieve more, even the toughest and most resilient of us can feel disheartened and defensive. It's not just our work, but our opinion of ourselves and our self-esteem that is challenged.

So, knowing this, what can we do to ease the feedback process and ensure that supervisory feedback will be both forthcoming and developmental? Ideally the feedback you receive will be considerately given and designed to help you grow as a researcher. We are aware from our own experiences, though, that not all doctoral students have access to this support, and not all exchanges of feedback are developmental and confidence building. Sometimes we have to guide others to give the feedback we need, and when we receive it, do our utmost to see the value and put aside our instincts to feel defensive.

Next we suggest a way that you could guide your supervisor to offer you the kind of feedback on progress that you can use. Even the most encouraging supervisor has many demands on their time and will appreciate knowing what you need from them. In return, ask them to advise you on their preferred methods and normal feedback turnaround times, for example, what is a reasonable response time for a short progress update compared to a longer piece of draft writing, or a presentation slide deck. In keeping with the rest of this chapter, use the following outline as an open process for discussion rather than being strictly bound by it.

- Record the actions you agreed to complete before the next meeting (as per the preceding meeting template) making sure, in writing, that you are all in agreement on the same list of what is to be achieved, and by when.
- Keep in touch on progress, provide short informal written updates to your supervisor(s) as tasks are completed. This can be as simple as an email back to everyone. Always include actions that cannot be completed, and what you have tried in order to overcome the obstacles arising. Attach artefacts of progress such as draft ethics proposals, chapters in progress, slide decks, or analysis files. Be honest if you have not started something, or if you have got stuck or confused and declare this to your supervisors. Hiding a lack of progress or points of confusion always creates problems later. Before sending it, reread what you have written and sense check the clarity and coherence of your informal progress report.
- When you send the update to your supervisor(s), offer some context about what exactly you are presenting for feedback. Do prioritise the parts you want to get feedback on and the kind of feedback you are looking for given the stage of the work – for example, is fine detail useful right now, or would you benefit from comments on the structure and sections of the work? You can make a request for how you ideally want to receive feedback too, for example verbally, as a recorded

audio or video message, or in writing. This guidance can save a supervisor time that could be lost trying to decipher what you have sent and where to start, and mean that you get feedback sooner and in a way you can use.

- Make time to discuss the feedback. Whether you choose to receive comments verbally in your next catch up, or in writing so that you can have time to process and understand it, feedback that is passively received is a job only half done. Understanding the rationale for the feedback, and how to use it to make a positive change, comes through engaging in dialogue. Ask questions if you don't understand. Don't forget to leave with clearly summarised actions as you begin the cycle again.

An ongoing process

All the advice we have offered in this chapter is intended to support you to engage in open conversations and build trust with your supervisor(s) as a gradual process of nego-tiation over time, so that the day-to-day reality of working together need not be so dramatic as to feel like a matter of "making or breaking" – a phrase with which we opened this chapter. If you make time to stop and reflect on how things are going, you will be able to find ways to continue to tailor and build the partnership.

Our intention in offering you these ideas is to challenge the idea of "one shot" thinking where all expectations are firmly set at the start of the doctorate and they can never change. We have also set out in this chapter to disrupt the idea that in supervision you "get what you are given" and are powerless to influence the partnership. A tailored approach benefits everyone, and for part-time researchers with complex identities and competing priorities, it is especially essential. It may be that you came into this chapter looking for ways you might make changes for the positive, and we hope you have found our ideas supportive of that too. We encourage you to work with your supervisor in an open way going forward. Over time, as the supervisory partnership and its patterns become established and then cemented, you may find that persisting with a supervision relationship that is not working well has cost you more time and energy to navigate than the effort of a conversation that addresses this directly. We encourage you to collaborate with your supervisor on a better way forward. Occasionally though, despite your best efforts, a better way forward with them may not be possible. It may benefit you to instead consider a change of supervisor (see also Chapter 8). To manage this process, before deciding who to approach, or reaching out to the relevant people to discuss your options, do some preparatory thinking. Consider what you have learned so far about yourself, your doctoral journey, the supervision that will support you to be at your best, and the types of relationships or behaviours that prevent you from working well.

It is worth saying explicitly, as a final remark, that it is not your responsibility to bear the effects or to change the behaviour of a supervisor who engages in toxic behaviour. We have seen many unfortunate cases of researchers whose emails go unanswered, whose thesis chapters stagnate in in-trays for months, or who are refused face-to-face time for meetings. If you aren't getting appropriate support or feedback from your supervisor(s), and you try the preceding ideas, it's a good idea to raise this as an issue with the designated staff member for doctoral student matters in your deparment. You may find this through other members of your supervisory team, your departmental PGR tutor (convenor), director of graduate studies, graduate school, PGR administrator, researcher development colleagues, central student support teams, students' union, or trade union. Our advice sits on top of the fundamental and non-negotiable expectation that you have the right in law not to be bullied or harassed by a supervisor or anyone else. If you are experiencing behaviour that is undermining, threatening, coercive, or is affecting your physical or mental health, we encourage you to seek support as soon as possible.

What you have discovered in this chapter would make a useful addition to your "route map" created in Chapter 2. We suggest that you revisit your map and continue to annotate it, based on your learning in each subsequent chapter.

Researchers recommend ...

- Consider what you want from a supervisor, or supervisory team. Thinking this through for yourself will help you to articulate it. You have a stake in shaping your supervision and in co-creating the partnership with your supervisors.
- Think carefully about the different contributions supervisors can make, and the limitations of the supervisor role. Avoid assumptions and myths and communicate your preferences openly.
- Approach your supervisory relationships as an ongoing partnership in which you need to be an active player, negotiate, and compromise.

References

Albertyn, R. and Bennett, K. (2021) 'Containing and harnessing uncertainty during postgraduate research supervision'. *Higher Education Research & Development*, 40(4), 661–675. doi: 10.1080/07294360.2020.1775559

Australian Council of Graduate Research, (2021) 'Good Practice Guidelines for Quality Graduate Research Supervision'. Available at: https://www.acgr.edu.au/wp-content/uploads/2021/08/ACGR-Guidelines-for-Quality-Graduate-Resesarch-Supervision.pdf

Bryan, B. and Guccione, K. (2018) 'Was it worth it? A qualitative exploration of graduate perceptions of doctoral value'. *Higher Education Research and Development*, 37(6), 1124–1140. doi: 10.1080/07294360.2018.1479378

Guccione, K. (2018) *Trust Me! Building and breaking professional trust in doctoral student-supervisor relationships. Project Report*. Leadership Foundation for Higher Education, London, UK.

Jacobsen, M., Friesen, S. and Becker, S. (2021) 'Online supervision in a professional doctorate in education: Cultivating relational trust within learning alliances', *Innovations in Education and Teaching International*, 58(6), 635–646. doi: 10.1080/14703297.2021.1991425

Lee, A. (2008) 'How are doctoral students supervised? Concepts of doctoral research supervision', *Studies in Higher Education*, 33(3), 267–281.

Rainford, J. (2020) 'Personal, social and disciplinary connectors: the part-time, long-haul supervisor'. Available at: https://supervisingphds.wordpress.com/; https://supervisingphds.wordpress.com/2020/09/14/personal-social-and-disciplinary-connectors-the-part-time-long-haul-supervisor/

UK Council for Graduate Education. (2019) The Good Supervisory Practice Framework. Available at: https://supervision.ukcge.ac.uk/good-supervisory-practice-framework/

Whittington, K., Barnes, S., and Lee, A. (2021) in Lee, A. and Bongaart, R. *The future of doctoral research: Challenges and opportunities*. Routledge, Abingdon, UK.

5 Managing your project

By the end of this chapter, you will

- Be able to consider how effective planning approaches can support your doctorate.
- Have considered a range of approaches and tools for planning and which might work best for you and your project.
- Have a better understanding of the importance of a planning approach that considers not just the thesis but also personal and work life together.

What's in store

Doctorates can be daunting for various reasons. Like anything that is designed to challenge you, the end goal often seems far away and unmanageable. The aim of this chapter is to help you consider how to take your thoughts from Chapter 2 and turn them into a workable plan that helps keep you on track. It will allow you to think through what to include in your plan and consider tools that might support the planning process.

DOI : 10.4324/9781003223931-6

Real-world reflection – fitting in the part-time doctorate

Dr Melanie Simms completed her PhD in 2006 from Cardiff University, researching trade union organising with a focus on how we evaluate effectiveness and sustainability of organising campaigns. You can find her on Twitter: @SimmsMelanie. Here she reflects upon how to fit your project in around other commitments.

My main lesson from the PhD was how to fit research in around the "edges" of other responsibilities. The activities of research break down into slightly different sets of tasks that need to be dealt with differently.

1. Work out when you can do particular tasks
I am an early bird and mornings are the best for concentrated tasks. For me, writing must be a morning task. At latest, before lunch. General admin, contacting research participants, and editing can all be done after noon. I cannot work in the evening. I'd rather go to bed early and get up an hour earlier, than work in the evening.

2. [My] Writing is slow
I love writing, but I am slow. Five hundred words a day tops, especially academic work for publication. For writing I need to be at my most alert. So, writing something in the hour before I open my emails is essential. It doesn't suit everyone but does me.

3. Editing takes time

I find this easiest in the afternoon. I think of it as a patchwork blanket where my first job is to make the sections. Then I can arrange them into a structure that makes sense and can spend time carefully "sewing" them together with links, summarising paragraphs, and signposting.

4. Some things that don't feel like work are work

At the start of a new topic, it is always hard to get to grips with a new literature. It often demands close reading of texts which I can only really do when I'm fresh in the morning. However, getting to grips with a topic can also come from conferences, seminars, and chats with friends and colleagues.

5. Travel time is useful

Time on the train to reflect after a conference or event is a central part of deeply immersing myself in ideas. I've learned not to schedule work during those train journeys! Long journeys are also often valuable for data analysis or thinking about what the data is trying to tell me.

6. My diary is my most important tool

To manage all these tasks and optimise my time, diary planning helps me a lot – if it's in my diary, I will do it.

Adapted from her original blog post:
https://thrivingparttime.com/2021/01/11/
finding-the-time-to-complete-a-part-time-phd/

Activity: Planning for known and unknown futures

All project management is based on assumptions. You will never know for certain what is around the corner, and you certainly cannot plan for every eventuality. When it comes to the part-time doctorate, add in an extended timeline and competing work and life commitments and this becomes even more challenging. In Chapter 2, you identified where you want to go with your doctorate and what you wanted from the experience. Hopefully, then, you have an idea of some of the things you need to do on the way.

Using those reflections from Chapter 2, try to pull out any things that you might need to build into your plans for the next 12 months. For example:

- Are there any conferences you want to attend?
- Do you have any formal academic requirements to complete?
- Do you want to get some wider experience to support your future goals?

These are the sort of things that are not usually asked for in formal plans for a research project but are equally important for your holistic development.

List anything that you might need to build into your planning for the next 12 months that is not in any existing plan you might have already developed.

Finally, add a list of things that might potentially be on the horizon. You are not a fortune teller, but for example there might be big life events that could throw a curve ball to your plans. Equally, you may have other commitments that potentially create immovable barriers you are going to need to contend with. After all, forewarned is forearmed!

Treating the doctorate as a project

There are many ways to plan a project. From formal, taught methods you might be familiar with like Gannt charts; methodologies such as PRINCE2 or Agile; or even a series of to-do lists scribbled on scraps of paper. Finding what works for you is often as much about trial and error as it is following a how-to guide. As previous research has found, doctoral researchers often have little training in project management (Katz, 2016). This does not mean you need to read all the literature on project management or take a course in it, but thinking about the doctorate through a project-focused lens can help you maintain control over it. All projects are "messy" to some extent, and from talking to doctoral students and graduates across disciplines and modes of study, most experience the doctorate as less linear than they expect. This means that plans must be both structured AND flexible.

Who controls your project?

It is worth pausing to consider all the people involved in your project. Whilst the doctorate can feel like a solo endeavour, it takes a village to raise a thesis as you will explore further in Chapter 7. Some of those involved are obvious, such as your supervisors. Others might be less so and vary based on the nature of the project. Some we came up with might be:

- Colleagues
- Participants
- Family
- Ethics committee
- Examiners

- Graduate School
- Reviewers (if you are writing for publication)

This means that there might be elements of your project that are reliant on another person completing a task that you have no control over. When this does not follow your plan, it can be a huge source of stress. There are several possible strategies to address this. Firstly, allow plenty of time in your plan for activities that are reliant on others – longer than you hope something will take. Secondly, have other tasks to occupy your time so you are not sitting waiting. There are always tasks you can be completing, but you need to know what these are so you have something to focus on.

Failing to keep to your plan can be a huge source of anxiety for doctoral researchers. We would argue that it doesn't have to be. Plans are great. They can help you see a way to your goals and the steps you need to get there. However, in most cases, plans are something you formulate yourself (maybe with guidance or based on external constraints, but they should be yours). One of the most useful pieces of advice that Jon found was in Elizabeth Day's (2020:14) book *Failosophy*. She frames plans as "an objective solution to a subjective problem" and goes on to highlight the problem with long-term plans is that you never really know what life is going to throw at you. Sometimes plans need to be adjusted and that's OK. Jon could not have anticipated redundancy and bereavement during the doctorate. Both of these required him to adapt and refocus. However, he put his energy into reworking the plans rather than panicking that he was not where the Gannt chart he carefully crafted in the proposal said he should be. Day also cites a quote from Eckhart Tolle that resonates here: 'The primary cause of unhappiness is never the situation but your thoughts about it' (Tolle cited in Day, 2020:39).

That said, there can be huge barriers that are not easily overcome through planning. In some contexts, there may be much bigger barriers to success that are beyond your control. As Rabe et al. (2021) highlight, in Nigeria, regular interruptions from strike action are a common feature of doing a doctorate. Similarly, violence in Colombian universities can also be a regular but unpredictable disruption (Tutkal et al., 2021). Additionally, the coronavirus pandemic has caused unpredictable delays and obstacles for many doctoral researchers over the past few years. Yet despite these huge challenges, many researchers can and do successfully complete their doctorates (often with reframing or replanning). Take solace in this because however bad it may seem at the time, most challenges do have an eventual solution.

Planning holistically

The doctorate

If you are coming to this book having already begun your doctoral journey, some of your planning may already have taken place. You may have been asked to submit a proposal with timelines in it. If you are doing a PhD by publication, you might already have some publications under your belt. In contrast, you may be coming to this before you have embarked on your doctoral journey. What this chapter is not going to do is take you through planning your project itself. If you want some support with that, we recommend Williams and Bethell (2010), *Planning your PhD*, or Firth, Connell and Freestone (2021), *Your PhD Survival Guide*.

Instead, we want to focus upon the many dependencies in the doctorate. There can be times where the project stalls due to waiting for feedback, permissions, access, respondents, experiments … You name it, there is probably a way it might stop you in your tracks. The key to this not impeding your progress is to anticipate these roadblocks and to have other tasks you can focus on whilst you are waiting.

We cannot emphasise enough that the doctorate is about far more than the thesis. A doctorate involves a range of training, practices, and activities that need to be juggled (Dowling and Wilson, 2017). If you are doing a taught doctorate, there will often be assignments to complete or practical assessments. You might also have aspects of the project that require you to complete some additional training, or career goals that mean you also want to gain wider experience during the doctorate. All of these things that you considered in the activities in Chapter 2 need to feature in your plan.

The thesis

When you think about your doctorate, the thesis is probably the biggest weight on your shoulders. For most doctoral researchers, it is the longest piece of writing you will have completed. It is also, like any form of writing, something that will be written, rewritten, edited, re-edited, polished, and revised numerous times. The reason we highlight this is that it is not a task that can just be "done." It is a project in itself. You might have chapters you write concurrently, or one chapter being read by a supervisor while you work on another. This means time needs to be spent considering how you might approach this.

A word of advice from the wise here. We hear time and time again from stressed out doctoral students that they wish they had factored in more time for formatting and polishing their references. If you can plan for this now, you will save a lot of stress later. We also both are huge advocates for investing the time in getting to grips with a referencing management software such as EndNote or Zotero. You may find it does not work for you, but for both of us it reduces a lot of stress.

Working around commitments

The doctoral journey is not linear for anyone. Throw in managing a career (and a life!) alongside this and there is the potential for a very winding road ahead. Every job and life have pinch points. For example, working in education, there are months where getting any quality time to focus on a doctorate can be impossible. Rather than stress and worry about this, try to factor it into your project. For taught doctorates, this may be trickier when there are set deadlines for assignments. Even for other types of doctoral researchers, annual review processes can often come at inconvenient times. However, these do tend to be predictable, so building time for these when it works best for you can be a useful strategy. For example, if you know your annual review paperwork is due in June but this is a hectic month, maybe plan ahead and block out some time in May.

The other thing to consider is the others on this journey with you. Try to ensure you plan quality time to maintain those relationships. To understand who others have found have helped their journeys, read any thesis acknowledgements and you will see the same can be said about a doctorate (something Chapter 7 explores in one of its activities). When we have talked with doctoral researchers, work, the doctorate, and family are the three biggest commitments they mention juggling. Even with the most supportive network, you can feel like you are not devoting enough time to them. By regularly scheduling days to do fun things together, this can take some of the pressure off those concerns and will also give you some well-needed space from the doctorate. How often is up to you, but as with anything, making a commitment can ensure this is given equal importance to all the other plates you are juggling.

Life planning

You will have probably heard the mantra that life is what happens while you are busy making other plans. In planning for life to happen alongside the doctorate, you are likely to come through the process happier, less resentful, and feeling more accomplished. There are a number of aspects of life to consider, both the expected and the unexpected. Whilst we cannot plan for the unexpected, we can put in leeway and time to account for the inevitable. After all, a part-time doctorate is a long endeavour and life happens. These things all have a time cost in terms of unexpected responsibilities but also an emotional cost that needs to be factored in.

We are both big believers in the idea that what gets scheduled in your diary becomes a commitment. How many of you regularly say "Oh, I must go to the gym this week" and then that never happens? However, if you make an appointment in your diary, you are much more likely to stick with that. Prioritise *YOU* as much as work and your thesis and we promise that the process will be far more pleasurable. Chapter 6 will focus specifically on how to ensure you have a good balance and exactly why it is important, but for now it is important to ensure you plan time for all those important things: Caring responsibilities, life administration, family occasions, hobbies, and holidays/vacations (yes, we encourage you to have these!).

Finding your ideal rhythm

When we have talked to part-time doctoral researchers, everyone seems to have their unique strategies for working on the doctorate. For most researchers, it is about carving out regular times that work for them. It is not uncommon for this to either fall early in the morning (kudos to those who can function at 4 am!) or late at night (equally, those burning the midnight oil have our respect). It does not need to be this extreme, though; it might be an hour or two before work, or a couple of hours after the children are asleep. What is important is protecting that time and staying consistent. Trying to find whole days or weeks to focus on a thesis can be an impossible task, but blocking out a focused hour or so is often more manageable.

For those of you juggling teaching or academic careers with the doctorate, blocks of full-time focus may be your friend, especially if you have a more seasonal work schedule. What is important here is to remember that within those blocks of time, breaking it down to keep the energy high is important. This might mean planning for a variety of tasks each day or other activities (more on this in Chapter 6). One way Jon did this in his doctorate towards the end, and still does with big writing projects like this, was to book mini-writing retreats. A couple of days with focused blocks of writing and breaks. It is amazing just how much you can get done sometimes when you remove outside distractions.

Creating and keeping on top of your plan

Juggling all the different aspects of the doctorate is hard for anyone. For the part-timer, adding in work commitments, life commitments, and activities to maintain a sense of well-being and it can become a lot to keep on top of. There are several technologies that might help you. However, there is not one ideal solution, so part of the process is about finding what works for you in your current situation.

Methods not tools

There are so many technological solutions out there to manage projects, it can often feel overwhelming to decide where to start. Dowling and Wilson (2017), in their study of PhD candidates' use of digital tools, highlighted that time, scepticism, and immediate utility can be barriers to their use by doctoral researchers. Whilst every tool claims to be a magic bullet for all your project needs, you will probably find you can achieve most of what you need to with existing tools. Jon is a big fan of digital tools; in fact, part of his career has been to support academics using technology. However, he struggled to make some of the bespoke project management apps work for him and often reverted to more traditional methods. He used a few tools but at the heart was a digital calendar that drew his personal, work, and study accounts into one. This was then supplemented with visual timelines and to-do lists in his office on a whiteboard using an adapted Kanban method.

What we would recommend is having an open mind and exploring different approaches and tools to find the ones that work for you. Talking to others in your support village can help you identify possibilities. Yet whether you use digital tools or not, at its most basic, managing a project is about ensuring all your tasks get done on time and in the right order. How you keep on top of that is up to you. At the heart of even the most bespoke pieces of software there are two main methods that underpin their functionality that are worth exploring a bit further here: Gannt charts and the Kanban method.

Gannt chart

At its essence, a Gannt chart is a way of visually representing how long a task will take, when it will begin and end, and what other tasks it overlaps with. The Gannt chart is a common feature of many approaches to project planning, and you will even see it used as a way to structure common software tools such as Asana and Monday. com. Many researchers choose to use excel to create simple Gannt charts due to its familiarity. Microsoft (2022) even offers a step-by-step guide.

Kanban

Having its origins in agile project management, the Kanban board (https://www.atlassian.com/agile/kanban/

boards) is a way to visualize tasks to be done, in progress, and completed. They can vary in their complexity but essentially, they are about making things visible. In a team this can be to show others but for the doctoral student this might just be a good way to keep on top of what you are currently juggling. *Trello* is a software tool that takes a digital approach to this method but equally it can be used on paper or a white board.

Key aspects include columns or workflows. Jon uses a simple approach of to-do, in progress, and under review for his writing projects. For your purposes, you might want columns for different aspects of your project. Perhaps with separate in-progress columns for admin, writing, and fieldwork tasks. You can also create rules for yourself if they help, such as no more than a certain number of tasks in progress, or by appending deadlines to the tasks. Like any of these methods, creative adaptation is likely to help them work better for you.

The good old to-do list

Whilst we have talked a lot about long-term project management here, there are also the day-to-day tasks that need to be managed. There is a lot to be said for the traditional to-do list. In fact, at this moment, Jon can see at least three of these from his desk. He tends to separate out his teaching, personal, and project-specific tasks into different lists. One of the challenges of the to-do list can be the size of the tasks. For example, one task is "mark assignments." This task could take a number of days and seems daunting; hence it has probably been avoided more than once. By breaking your tasks down into smaller chunks, it can make these lists more useful and easier to engage with. After all, how do you eat an elephant? One bite at a time! There are also tools that use a to-do list format and can help you think of it in different ways; the notes app in your phone can be a good way to keep tasks organised. *Workflowy* is a slightly more dynamic version of this. You can find a really good overview written in Firth (2017).

How do current doctoral researchers manage their projects?

In talking to current researchers on Twitter in 2021, some of the most popular bespoke project management tools were Trello, Asana, and Monday.com. By the time you are reading this, there may be new offerings. What was interesting was that more traditional methods such as physical lists, diaries, and more mainstream software like Excel and electronic calendars were often their primary mode of project management.

Real-world reflection – using a research diary

Dr Julia Everitt completed her Doctorate in Education at Staffordshire University in 2018. Julia's research drew on 100 years of educational policy to explore the rationales and ideologies behind external providers, agencies, and organisations working in four case study schools to support learning and well-being. You can connect with her on Twitter @juliaeverittdr. Here she reflects on the value of a research diary:

> Undertaking research is complex, messy, and not as linear as suggested by the timeline of

activities we outline in project Gantt charts. During my doctorate, there were twists and turns as I made decisions around which literature to include and which theoretical approaches to apply. Furthermore, my personal life was complex and messy – six years is a long time (during which we moved house and lost family members). My research diaries were a way to maintain connections between particular aspects of my thinking and activities whilst navigating the messiness of life. Some of the ways I used them were as follows:

- To keep track of **literature themes and visual interpretations**. I was able to revisit my interpretations as I read other literature to synthesise and make connections.
- Exploring **emerging theoretical frameworks**. I made notes and visual interpretations of theorists' views of society. Over time connections emerged that were important in the development of my thesis.
- Recording **supervisor interactions**. I would take my research diary to my supervision meetings and draw on it to discuss my progress, in addition to printing out key email communications.
- Keeping track of my **learning from events and networks**. I attended events, workshops, and conferences run by professional associations (e.g., BERA, SRHE), and at my own and other universities. I attended events around viva preparation, publishing, and academic writing

and have revisited these notes at different time points.

- Making sense of my **methodological dilemmas**. As it took a year to collect the data from my case study schools it would have been easy to forget some of the actions I took and my thoughts at the time. These were important in the later thesis and ensured thoughts were not lost over time.
- Documenting my **analysis**. I used the diary to keep track of my coding structures and their development. It can be easy to miss connections, and using a diary helped me track this over the extended period of the part-time doctorate.

My diaries are numbered and in date order so I can go back to any point easily to find my interpretations of an article, policy, or theory. This is helpful when lives are complex when we are juggling work, a part-time doctorate, and personal life. The diaries make it easy to pick up where I left off the last time.

Adapted from her original blog post:
https://thrivingparttime.com/2021/03/15/
my-research-diary-recording-the-twists-and-
turns-of-a-part-time-doctorate/

Activity: Prioritising demands on your time

As this chapter highlighted, you are likely to have a range of commitments you need to manage alongside each other. Whilst you may have been asked to make a timeline for your thesis or your research projects, it is likely this is a standalone document and only focused upon the research part of the puzzle.

In this activity we want you to think about your time more holistically:

1) **Using the headings doctorate, work, self, and family, write a list of all the commitments you have over the next 12 months**. Are there any big family events? Work pinch points? Days out? Holidays? Anniversaries? – The key here is to get everything down on a sheet of paper without over thinking it.

2) **Try to place these commitments into a chronological order** – Notice any potential overlaps. Some of these might mean you need to make compromises, but with some planning you might be able to adjust some of the deadlines. It is certainly easier to consider this at an early stage rather than having a panic at the last minute.

3) **Do any of these commitments require you to prepare for them?** If so, could this be easier with a planning tool either in isolation or as part of a more comprehensive "life" plan.

4) **Take some time to trial one of these methods in this chapter** – Use your research diary to reflect upon what works for you. This will help you identify other options to explore. For example, Jon liked the layout of Trello but not the software, so created his own on a whiteboard with magnetic labels. You might want to try different methods for different tasks to find out what works best for you.

It is also worth taking a moment to reflect upon what you have discovered in this chapter that would make a useful addition to your "route map" created in Chapter 2. We suggest that you revisit your map and continue to annotate it, based on your learning in this chapter.

Researchers recommend ...

- Managing your doctorate is about more than the thesis. Time invested early on in thinking about the project holistically will allow you to create more realistic plans.
- Always remember to add some leeway for life to throw you a curve ball. Future you will thank you for this!
- Try out a range of different tools to find what works for you. This might change over time as the number of plates you are juggling changes. There is no right way to do this, but working in short blocks of time and distraction-blocking apps may help.
- Use your plan to guide you but equally do not stress if you deviate from the original plan. Regularly review where you are and replan the next stages as needed. Your plan is primarily for you and no one else. At the end of the day, it is your best guess about an unknown future.

Where can I find out more?

Especially in terms of managing the final year of your project, Katherine Firth, Liam Connell, and Peta Freestone's *Your PhD survival guide: Planning, writing and succeeding in your final year* is like to be a great source of inspiration and practical support. Some of you reading this chapter might be considering careers where projects form a significant part. If this is the case, it may be worth investing time in exploring some of the project management literature.

References

Day, E. (2020) *Failosophy: A Handbook for When Things Go Wrong*, London: 4th Estate.

Dowling, R., & Wilson, M. (2017) 'Digital doctorates? An exploratory study of PhD candidates' use of online tools', *Innovations in Education and Teaching International*, 54(1), 76–86. doi:10.1080/14703297.2015.1058720

Firth, K. (2017) 'Yet another to-do list blog'. Available at: https://researchinsiders.blog/2017/04/10/yet-another-to-do-list-blog/

Firth, K., Connell, L., & Freestone, P. (2021) *Your PhD survival guide: Planning, writing and succeeding in your final year*, Abingdon: Routledge.

Katz, R. (2016) 'Challenges in doctoral research project management: A comparative study', *International Journal of Doctoral Studies*, 11, 105–125. Available at: http://ijds.org/Volume11/IJDSv11p105-125Katz2054.pdf

Microsoft (2022) 'Present your data in a Gantt chart in Excel', *Microsoft Support*. Available at: https://support.microsoft.com/en-us/topic/present-your-data-in-a-gantt-chart-in-excel-f8910ab4-ceda-4521-8207-f0fb34d9e2b6 (Accessed 12 April 2022).

Rabe, M., Agboola, C., Kumswa, S., Linonge-Fontebo, H., & Mathe, L. (2021) 'Like a bridge over troubled landscapes: African pathways to doctorateness', *Teaching in Higher Education*, 26(3), 306–320. doi:10.1080/13562517.2021.1896490

Tutkal, S., Busnelli, V., Castelao-Huerta, I., Barbosa dos Santos, F., Loaiza Orozco, L. F., & Rivera Arcila, D. (2021) 'Inhabiting borders: Autoethnographic reflections of PhD students in Colombia', *Teaching in Higher Education*, 26(3), 321–339. doi:10.1080/13562517.2021.1895108

Williams, K., & Bethell, E. (2010) *Planning your PhD*, London: Palgrave.

6 Finding your balance

By the end of this chapter, you will

- Understand how developing balance within the doctorate can improve your productivity.
- Have explored a range of tools and techniques for maintaining balance and focus.
- Identified which strategies you could put into practice to ensure you have balance in your life.

What's in store

We all know self-care is important. The problem is that when we get stressed and have a never-ending list of tasks, doing things for ourselves often feels like a luxury we cannot afford. In this chapter we will explain why making time for you and finding your balance will make you more productive (Yes, it will, trust us!). We will help you consider what types of activities work well both within your own constraints and to act as much-needed downtime. The chapter will show you in practice exactly how taking breaks can help you make those breakthroughs in your thinking and writing.

DOI : 10.4324/9781003223931-7

Real-world reflection – making the most of your time

Dr Nicole Brown undertook her part-time PhD at the University of Kent, examining academic identities under the influence of fibromyalgia. It drew on a range of social science disciplines across sociology and education. You can connect with her on Twitter @ncjbrown. Here she highlights her relationship with time.

> If I was to summarise the main concern and the main advantage of my experience of a part-time doctorate, it would be that time flies and stands still, at the same time.
>
> **Time is precious**
> Of course, time is precious for every student, but if you must cram studying, reading, researching, marking, teaching, planning, supporting colleagues, school runs, cooking, household chores, and any other family commitments into your day, your time becomes even more precious. My day became a slick military operation of managing time; no time was ever wasted. If I needed to wait for a few minutes somewhere, I would use that time to be productive by reading and highlighting or making notes.
>
> **A day lost is not a lost day**
> When it came to the weeks and months of field research, I noticed my full-time colleagues worrying and panicking if there were delays with the ethics forms or when interviews needed to

be rescheduled. A day lost was indeed a full day lost. In my case, rescheduling a day wasn't really a full day lost. I was "only" a part-time student, so in terms of equivalencies a full day lost only for them converted into a half-day loss for me. And if there was more time at risk, then I focused on work commitments and crammed all that into my days and traded those for PhD days a few weeks later. Catching up with days lost felt easier to manage for me than for the full-timers.

Time to take a break

Because of that stretchability of the day being a half-day that can be made up easily, I think I took more breaks from my doctorate than the full-time students did. Like I said earlier, having a break from the PhD did not mean idling my time away; I had other things to do. But it did mean that I had time away from the doctoral study and the brain work involved with that. Any break I took or had to take from my PhD became a deliberate rest. For some people, deliberate rest may be taking time for exercise or arts and craft activities; for me, it meant dealing with the other tasks and commitments in my life. The benefit of such a deliberate rest is that your brain has time to process and mull things over and when you come back to the problem, you will be better equipped to focus and find solutions.

Adapted from her original blog post: https://thrivingparttime.com/2021/02/01/ the-part-time-doctorate-when-time-flies-and-stands-still/

Activity: How does this chapter relate to me?

Drawing back on the plans you created in the last chapter, make a list of all your commitments in three columns – must / should / would like to

We would predict that many of you will have most of the "fun" things you like to do in the would like to column.

Some questions to reflect upon:

- Why are the activities in that category?
- Who set the priority for that activity and why?
- Would making a particular activity a higher priority improve your sense of well-being?

Quite often we prioritise those things that others place importance on as opposed to what is important for us. This chapter is going to explore how to address that balance.

A note about "shoulds." A should is often an assumption you make about yourself. Check they are definitely "shoulds" and not just expectations that other people put upon you. It is worth taking some time to reflect upon this and keep it under review over time.

What this chapter is not

This chapter is focused on creating a balance and thinking about how to make the doctorate work for your life and circumstances. What we are not attempting to do is provide a support guide specifically for well-being. There is another volume in this series by Petra Boynton (2021), *Being Well in Academia*, that we would recommend as a complement to this book. However, there is some synergy between what we will explore in this chapter and Boynton's work. Ideas such as prioritising self-care and creating support networks are central to this book's approach.

We also cannot solve all your problems or make your distractions go away. Many distractions, especially digital ones, can be minimised, but people and real-world distractions are more challenging. It is also a reality that we all have commitments that often need to take priority. What we will do in this chapter is offer strategies for working around these to try and reduce their negative impact upon your success.

The "on fire" doctoral triangle

You may remember from when you were at school that you learnt about the "fire triangle." This is a diagram that demonstrates what is needed for fire to occur: fuel, oxygen, and heat. When things are going well in the doctorate, it often feels like a fire burning brightly. Like an actual fire,

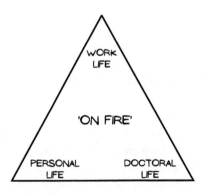

Figure 6.1 The "on fire" doctoral triangle

to be "on fire" with your doctoral journey you also need to have three elements working well for you: Personal life, work life, and doctoral life.

It is easy to let your doctorate take over your personal life. Equally, it is also easy for paid, unpaid, or caring work to overtake the doctorate. Both situations are a recipe for potential stress and anxiety. When they are out of balance, this can have a negative impact upon your well-being. It is therefore important to keep this image in your mind when thinking about how you might balance the different aspects of all three.

Activity: Do you have balance?

On a piece of paper, start by listing all the demands you have on your time under three headings: Doctorate / Work (paid and unpaid) / Personal Life

Do not think too much to start with, just get down as much as you can. You are going to be using this list to think about balance in your time and managing priorities.

Some questions to consider:

- How are these demands spread?
- Which columns put the most demand on your time?
- Why might that be?
- How might rebalancing them impact upon your life?

This can be a really good way to think about what might need some attention.

Now look specifically at the personal life category. How many of those things allow you to have some time for yourself? If the answer here is few or none, this might be something to reflect upon as we will return to it later in the chapter.

Managing your time (and your distractions!)

How many times have you sat at a computer "trying" to be productive? We certainly are both guilty of that, especially when we might have blocked out a day to write for example. No matter how much you stare at that screen though, the words often don't come. This in turn, can frustrate us more and lead to a cycle of unproductivity. It may seem counterintuitive but for many of you, working less may lead to better progress. We are going to first look at some techniques that are commonly used by doctoral researchers to maximise their focus before exploring the value of breaks.

Pomodoro

One of the most commonly used time management techniques is the pomodoro technique. Developed by Francesco Cirillo, the term comes from the Italian word for tomato, after the tomato shaped kitchen timer that is traditionally used. Simply put, the pomodoro technique involves blocking your work to 25-minute chunks with five-minute breaks between. This technique is about getting to know how long tasks take, to create space for reflecting upon progress and next steps, and for blocking out distractions. Cirillo argues that these more intensely focused bursts can help you better organise your work and create more free time (Cirillo, 2022).

Whilst these 25-minute bursts are the traditional method, you can use the principles of blocking out your time and working in chunks in whatever way works for you. Have a particularly meeting-littered day? What about 10- or 15-minute chunks instead? Trying to do a task that requires a longer period? What about a 55-minute block and a longer break? The beauty is that the concept of working in bursts of time can be adapted to your situation (just remember to take those breaks!).

There's an app for that

One of the key principles of the pomodoro technique is blocking out a chunk of focused time. How often have you thought, "oh, I'll do this task this afternoon" and then the doorbell rings, or the world seems to be falling apart around you, or you just go to check for something online and fall into a world of cat videos (surely, it's not just us?). As well-disciplined as we try to be, digital distraction is a real thing and sometimes we need help.

If you use a smart phone, many have focus modes now built into them that will mute notifications and other distractions. You might want to go further, and there are a number of both Windows and Mac compatible applications that can help. The basic premise of all of these is that they can block you from doing certain things on your devices or mute notifications for a period of time to help you focus. We recommend searching for "apps that help you focus" to find the best ones for you as there are new apps all the time. One of Jon's current favourites is *flow* (https://flowapp.info/) which also integrates a pomodoro-style timer system and allows you to block specific apps that you know are a distraction for you whilst allowing you access to others.

Writing together: Creating accountability

Arranging sessions for writing socially can be really help-ful. Not only does it offer accountability, but it can be a way to block out time in your diary to focus, which is sometimes needed to prevent other urgent things taking priority. If you want to organise your own groups there are some great resources on https://powerhourofwriting. wordpress.com/the-power-hour-of-writing/, which draw on Rowena Murray's (2015) *Writing in social spaces*. For those of you who prefer to work alone or do not have a group of people in similar situations, you can also find recorded videos of people working, which often incorpo-rate the pomodoro technique. We have heard from some doctoral researchers that this is also helpful to improve their focus.

Quiet email boxes

Many of us are slaves to our emails. As a part-time doc-toral researcher, I would guess you have at least three email accounts if not more. We are sure that lots of you also have these constantly connected, receiving notifica-tions to your smart devices or computer inbox for every email. We would also guess that many of you have these programs open in the background when you are working on a computer. If not, well done, you can probably ignore this next paragraph.

If you are a slave to your email, being more mindful of how you engage with it can really help with balance. Rarely is an email so urgent it cannot wait a few hours, yet when they ping in, the temptation to deal with things quickly can be high, especially when we are overloaded. You also do not want to use your best energy triaging and dealing with admin tasks. For some readers, mornings may not be your most productive time. If so, this might be an ideal time to do email. If mornings are your most productive, try to avoid email for the first two hours to focus on writing or tasks that require your best self (when Jon was a doctoral researcher, this was his thesis time).

A quiet inbox means only checking it at specific times of day. This might be once in the morning and once in the afternoon (or whatever works for you). You can also use this with the pomodoro technique to assign how long you are going to focus on your emails, leaving anything that does not get done until the next email hour. Each person's situation is likely to be different, so it is important to adapt this for your needs. However, the principle of being more mindful of the time you spend in the vortex of your inbox is the key point here.

Sometimes you need to unplug

One of the best ways to manage distractions can be to remove them completely. This is especially true when it comes to intense periods of writing. Different things work for different people, but Jon found that the competing demands on his time meant that a more extreme approach was needed. What worked for him was to spend a couple of days in a place with no internet connection. This forcibly removed the interruptions, both digital and those associated with being at home (including those chores and doorbell distractions that often open a gateway to other distractions). As he wrote, if there was something he might need to look up, he simply added notes to himself in the text to do this later. There are of course less extreme ways to do this. You might find it helps to go to a different place to write that does not have Wi-Fi, or to leave the phone at home.

Managing real-world distractions

The elephant in the room here is often literally in the room. Real-world distractions are often harder to escape than their digital relations. Sometimes the only way to avoid these is to remove them. This might mean finding somewhere different to work or being very firm on boundaries. Of course, this can be easier said than done and some things cannot just be moved. Three strategies that might help:

- **Be open and honest with people around you** – Often, they are just not aware that they are being a distraction. Try to explain what would help you, and if needed, negotiate time to do things together you enjoy.
- **Try to match activities with environments** – Some things you may need silence for, others it might be possible to do in small chunks with noise and distraction. If you have a selection of tasks on the go, it is easier to shift to something you can manage.
- **Create accountability** – This might be through social working or writing activities. If you struggle to carve out time to write, make it a meeting and work remotely with someone to keep each other accountable. This also gives you the permission to tell everyone you need peace because you are in a meeting.

Working out what really matters, right now

That perfect space and time to make a start on the thing you have been putting off may never come so sometimes you might need to make the task fit your situation. Try to break it down into parts. What might you be able to do in the 15-minute slot you have between meetings? What might you be able to do with that data in the car while you are waiting to pick up the children from afterschool club?

Often what can stop us making progress is this need for perfection or completion of one task before moving on. Even just managing to get some thoughts down with markers like [NEED TO FINISH THIS THOUGHT LATER] can be really helpful for having other things to pick up when you encounter similar short gaps in your schedule in future. There is always something you can do though, and being armed with an ongoing to-do list of bite-sized tasks can be one way to find something that will work in whatever specific situation you are in.

Work-life integration

Trying to fit what matters into a day can often mean juggling multiple plates. Whilst this chapter is called finding your balance; you might be expecting us to focus on a "work-life balance." However, we prefer the term work-life integration (Dresdale, 2016) as it sees work, life, family (and in your case the doctorate), as interrelated, overlapping, and often without clear differentiation. This contrasts with work-life balance, which assumes a distinct separation between work and life (Cheng-Tozun, 2018).

The way to integrate these elements is through consciously planning and managing these various elements. However, the danger of planning can be the temptation to try and fill every gap with "something." This leaves no wiggle room for the unexpected, or scope to deal with tasks that take longer than planned, ultimately resulting in stress and anxiety. Equally, when faced with a choice of which task to drop, we can be driven towards the urgent as opposed to the important.

Managing these demands is about aligning your needs with a set of competing demands from others such as friends, family, employers, and perhaps your supervisors. We say perhaps here, because in the process of becoming a doctoral researcher, we hope the agency will be shifting from one of being told what to do to one where you are driving your project. You need to ensure that you are focusing on your needs first. We can often say yes to things to please others, but the reality is if you are focused on others, it is hard to stay in control of what is important to you. Ellard (2015) argues that it is your choice to define what this balance is and how it might change over time. She suggests that imbalance often comes from not communicating with others (or being honest with ourselves!).

Creating boundaries

It can be very easy for a doctorate to take over your life. If you let it, it can be all consuming. There is also a tendency for academics to wear overwork as a badge of honour, which can fuel our need to feel like we are "doing more." However, creating boundaries is important. You are more than your thesis, but to enable you to integrate this with other demands and keeping physically and mentally well, you need to create boundaries. In some guides for full-time students, you might often see "treat it like a 9-to-5 job" as commonly shared advice to maintain balance. Obviously, for most part-time doctoral researchers this will not work as you already have other 9-to-5 commitments or health and caring needs that make this ineffective advice. Equally, this 9-to-5 model does not take full advantage of the idea of integration. However, it can be useful to think about how much time you can and should be devoting to your doctorate each week. Regularly devoting time to your project is likely to be more sustainable than overworking and suffering phases of burnout.

Boundaries do not have to be permanent. As Emma Reed-Turrell emphasises in an episode of the *Best Friend Therapy*, you can renegotiate them over time (Day and Reed-Turrell, 2022). Many people worry about setting boundaries based on letting others down, or fear that saying no to something might offend someone. However, as Reed-Turrell argues, by creating boundaries we are demonstrating we can take control, which can impress people.

Nonetheless, you should be prepared that your boundaries may sit uncomfortably with others. This can cause upset or frustration but again, Reed-Turrell astutely highlights that what other people do with their emotions in relation to boundaries you create is up to them. What is important is that you are taking actions that result in you maintaining a balance of what is important to you.

Boundaries might be around how many commitments you take on, whether you agree to a proposed deadline – or negotiate something that is likely to be more realistic in your current situation. They might also involve blocking out your diary for certain activities, commitments, or just simple down time. Setting boundaries might also involve saying "not now" to some opportunities that might be great but would throw you out of balance.

Take breaks, make breakthroughs

We all have different interests and ways to wind down. For some strange reason both the authors of this book enjoy running, swimming, and cycling a really long distance. For Jon, though, it is really the running and swimming where he feels he gets the most benefit. There is something about both of these that allow his mind to switch off, which is often when those breakthroughs happen. Now we are not promising you are going to make a Nobel prize–winning discovery, but often going out for a run has helped both of us find that phrase we were struggling to write or helping finally make sense of the data we were trying to analyse. Of course, this is not school, we aren't about to force you to go for a run around a wet boggy field (unless you want to!). When we talk to other researchers, we often hear them advocate other activities for the same reason. The ones we hear most often are knitting, crochet, sewing, painting, pottery, gardening, doing jigsaws, and walking. What all of these have in common is that they all involve repetitive action that can distract us. Sometimes accountability helps here. You can share what you are doing to create this balance using the #TakeBreaksMakeBreakthroughs on Twitter.

Use your diary for YOU

It is all very well and good for us to tell you to make time for these things, but anyone who has tried to make a new year's resolution will tell you that however good your intent, life often supersedes the things that we see as nice to do. The way we have both overcome this is to diarise these activities and give them as much prominence as any other meeting or task. In Chapter 5 we talked about managing your project and we would advocate making "project you" as important as "project thesis" in your holistic planning. This may also be easier said than done, so creating accountability with your support network (more on this in the next chapter!) is a great thing to do.

Creativity to find balance

Creativity can be another way to support balance. For example, Lazarus (2021) talks about how he used poetry as a coping mechanism in dropping out from his initial PhD programme and shifting to a PhD by publication in another. Similarly, Clare Daněk (2020) maintained a stitch journal during her doctorate (initially started full time and now part time) as a way of documenting her journey but also dealing with the emotions and the highs and the lows of navigating her research journey.

Health/dis(ability)

Part-time study is often a conscious choice for those of us living with long-term health conditions or disabilities. These might be part of the reason for wanting to work towards a doctorate; alternatively they might feel like a barrier to reaching that goal. Either way, we have both seen many researchers with a vast array of needs thrive during their doctorates.

Having additional challenges to navigate can mean that that you need to be more flexible in your plans, create more time for certain tasks, or plan around periods where you need to prioritise your health needs. Neither of us are specialists in this area and this book does not aim to offer specific support for individual needs (see some of the recommended readings at the end of this chapter). However, some of our top tips are as follows:

- Communicate your needs. We are sure you have successfully developed a whole raft of coping strategies to this stage of your academic career. Knowing what these are and how they can help reduce the load can be the difference between surviving and thriving in your doctorate.
- You are the expert on **YOU**. Whilst supervisors, support staff, and others who are there to help you on your journey may have had training or experience of working with people with similar conditions, we each have our own specific needs. Don't be afraid to communicate these to ensure they are met.
- Dealing with university support systems as a part-time researcher can be hard, especially if it is done at a distance. We would recommend, if you can, getting to know the people behind the services. If you already have a connection with them, trying to get help by email or phone can feel less like a barrier.
- You might need to build your health or disability needs into the project plan you develop. If you have a condition that has good or bad days, create that flexibility so you can work when you are feeling at full capacity rather than worrying you are falling behind.

- Be aware that your doctoral journey may be more convoluted than others. There is always more than one way to the finish and that might be specific to you. It might feel frustrating seeing others move at different paces, but as cliched as it sounds, the race is only with yourself.
- Finally, be kind to yourself! We talked earlier in the chapter about taking breaks. These breaks, depending on your condition might just be curling up on the sofa in a blanket (and that's OK!).

Caring

Caring may also be another aspect of your life that you need to juggle alongside the doctorate. This can range from parenting to caring for a partner or family member. Like health and disability needs, this can also be unpredictable and often throw a curve ball at the most inopportune of moments.

Sometimes it is important to remember that your doctorate is just a project, however much it seems to consume your life. It will still be there when the needs of those you are caring for are sorted. No one will ever think any less of you for prioritising these responsibilities, even if we sometimes feel like they would. As with our previous tips, communication here is key. You do not have to share everything, but it can often be a good idea to be open and honest with your supervisor as to how this might generally impact your research. Likewise, when unexpected events happen, being open and honest can be the key to finding a strategy to get through.

Real-world reflection – the importance of balance

Selina Griffin is undertaking a Doctorate in Education at the Open University. You can connect with her on Twitter @psylina. Her doctorate focuses on how/whether learning analytics can be used in a professional development organisation (Toastmasters) to improve retention. She has reflected on the importance of balance in her doctorate. Here are some of her top tips:

1. **Enjoy your study**

   You have to at this level. I'm not saying I always enjoy it obviously, particularly when I'm struggling with an assignment or grappling with a paper or a concept I can't figure out, but you need to be excited about what you are doing.

2. **Belong**

   Being a part-time researcher, you can struggle with your identity and your motivation. It can feel isolating and like something "extra" rather than who you are. You are just as much a researcher as someone who is full time. Own it and make it part of your identity (I put it in my signature after my job title and on Twitter!).

3. **Find your you**

   It is important to have something outside of your study. I do Toastmasters. I hug my cat. But I also exercise and run (including marathons). I run because it helps me to think. When you work at a computer, then study at a computer and its lockdown, I need a break!

4. **Balance**

I use running as a motivation (just read one more paper, then you can go for a run) or a tool to help me focus (now you've run you can study for a couple of hours) – the approach depends on the priority for the day and other commitments. This can apply to other hobbies too.

5. **Allow for Eureka moments**

It's a cliché, but I do think clearly when I run and a work or a study problem will often unpack itself and present a solution. Once I am back, I make notes. I have a Trello board for study, and I add cards to ensure I capture and remember key ideas or trains of thought as I come to them, for processing later.

Adapted from her original blog post: https:// thrivingparttime.com/2021/03/08/finding-balance-during-the-part-time-doctorate/

Activity: How can I apply this to my own doctorate?

This chapter has focused on thinking about how your life is currently balanced and what might need addressing. Going back to the earlier activity, did you have a good balance within your doctorate-work-personal triangle? How much of that personal life was set aside for you to recharge?

Take some time to consider the following questions:

- What activities allow you to switch off?
- When might you do these activities?
- How are you going to hold yourself accountable?

Physical reminders can be really helpful. Both Jon and Kay like to diarise their breaks. This may not work for you, but having visual cues to remind you to do some of these activities may be helpful. You can also think about making plans with others to help ensure you do some of these activities regularly. You might also want to think about how you can integrate these. Can you make some down time during the day, or within doctorate-focused sessions to break them up?

Before you move on from this chapter, commit to three things you are going to do to help improve the balance. You might want to share these commitments with other people to give yourself some additional accountability.

What you have discovered in this chapter would make a useful addition to your "route map" created in Chapter 2. We suggest that you revisit your map and continue to annotate it, based on your learning in each subsequent chapter.

Researchers recommend ...

- Making the best use of your time is the key to finding balance. Part of this is developing your awareness of what works for you. There is no point sitting at a computer if you are not achieving anything.
- Use tools to help you. This might be a diary or journal; it might be apps to help you focus. It might also be social media to share your successes and to get tips from other doctoral researchers.
- Place as much importance on making time for breaks and activities that allow you to replenish your energy

as much as you do work and research commitments. Remember to put on your oxygen mask before helping others.

Where can I find out more?

Health and disability needs might be something you want more support on. Your university's student support services is a good place to start, but there are a number of specialist resources and networks out there that might help. In some contexts these might include developing plans to support you. We also highly recommend Zoe Ayres's (2022) *Managing your Mental Health during your PhD: A Survival Guide*, as it will still have resonance for whatever type and mode of doctorate you are studying for.

A lot of the issues this chapter raises are not specific to the doctorate. You might want to look at podcasts and books that focus on balance more generally. *Best Friend Therapy*, which we reference in the chapter, is a great podcast for thinking about some of the psychology that underpins why we tend not to prioritise our own mental well-being.

References

Ayres, Z. J. (2022) *Managing your Mental Health during your PhD: A Survival Guide*. Cham, Switzerland: Springer Nature.

Boynton, P. (2021) *Being Well in Academia*, Abingdon: Routledge.

Cheng-Tozun, D. (2018) 'Work-Life Balance vs. Work-Life Integration: How Are They Different, and Which One Is for You?', *Inc*. Available at: https://www.inc.com/dorcas-cheng-tozun/how-work-life-integration-can-help-you-have-it-all.html (Accessed 12 April 2022).

Cirillo, F. (2022) 'The pomodoro technique', *Francesco Cirillo*. Available at: https://francescocirillo.com/pages/pomodoro-technique (Accessed 12 April 2022).

Daněk, C. (2020) 'Stitch Journal', *Clare Daněk thinking and making – research and creative practice*. Available at: https://claredanek.me/stitch-journal/ (Accessed 12 April 2022).

Day, E. and Reed-Turrell, E. (2022. March 28) Boundaries [audio podcast episode] In *Best Friend Therapy*. Apple Podcasts. https://podcasts.apple.com/gb/podcast/best-friend-therapy/id1614793299?i=1000555399900

Dresdale, R. (2016) 'Work-life balance vs. work-life integration, is there really a difference?', *Forbes*. Available at: https://www.forbes.com/sites/rachelritlop/2016/12/18/work-life-balance-vs-work-life-integration-is-there-really-a-difference/?sh=6243ecaa3727 (Accessed 12 April 2022).

Ellard, J. (2015) 'Can we stop talking about what to call work-life balance, *Huffington Post*. Available at: https://www.huffpost.com/entry/can-we-stop-talking-about-what-to-call-work-life-balance_b_8021232 (Accessed 12 April 2022).

Lazarus, S. (2021) 'Demonstrating the therapeutic values of poetry in doctoral research: Autoethnographic steps from the enchanted forest to a PhD by publication path', *Methodological Innovations*, 14(2). doi:10.1177/20597991211022014

Murray, R. (2015) *Writing in social spaces*, Abingdon: Routledge.

7   Building your village

By the end of this chapter you will

- Understand why having a range of people within your support network can help you on your doctoral journey.
- Have identified those relationships or networks that you might want to develop further.
- Have considered the best way to build and maintain your networks both online and offline.

What's in store

This chapter will help you consider how to develop support networks that work for you. It will explore the role of both online and physical opportunities for developing these connections. These connections can take many different forms, are based on your own plans for after the doctorate, and are likely to evolve over time. The chapter will therefore help you think about how networks can provide emotional and professional support that complements that provided through supervisors. It will also allow you to think about how to develop and maintain these networks to help with the isolation in the part-time doctorate.

DOI : 10.4324/9781003223931-8

Real-world reflection – who makes up a village?

Dr Jon Rainford completed his PhD in 2019 at Staffordshire University as a part-time researcher. You can find him on Twitter @jonrainford. His work focuses on policy and practice of widening participation in higher education. Here he reflects upon his own support village.[1]

One of the biggest revelations that I had as a doctoral student myself was that your doctorate is not a solo endeavour. After all, part of the goal of the doctorate is to enable you to become an independent researcher. However, the networks you build can be invaluable to helping you on this journey and feeling far less like you are lost at sea. They need to be both built and cultivated based on your own needs. After all, each researcher comes with distinct expertise, experiences, and areas for development, so the team of "Hidden Curriculum agents" (Elliot et al., 2020) that *you* need to support *your* progress to becoming an independent researcher can vary.

Everyone's village is likely to be different, but it might be helpful for you to see who was most influential in my own village as a part-time PhD researcher:

- **Supervisor**: Important but not my *only* form of support.
- **Administrative staff**: Building personal connections made getting help at a distance easier.

- **Doctoral peers in my institution**: Maintaining connections with peers was valuable when I needed to know who to talk to for various things related to the university.
- **Postgraduate subject networks**: Connections with other doctoral researchers was invaluable for the development of my thinking and ideas.
- **Academic colleagues**: They helped me to keep abreast of developments in the field and opportunities.
- **Work colleagues**: Having managers and colleagues that understood the undertaking of a doctorate and the pressures and stresses that can create was invaluable.
- **A trusted proofreader**: Someone who can help you with this allows your supervisors to focus on the content of the thesis rather than the typos.
- **Emotional support**: This was provided by my partner. But having someone to make me take breaks and give me an escape from the thesis was important, especially in the final stages.

Adapted from his original blog post:
https://drhiddencurriculum.wordpress.
com/2021/10/25/building-your-support-tribe/

Activity: Who inhabits the villages of other doctoral researchers?

The doctorate can often feel like a lone endeavour. However, every successful doctoral graduate will tell you of the army of people who have supported their journeys. In fact, you only have to read a few acknowledgements pages in other theses to realise how important people are to doctoral success. Gardner and Gopaul (2012) in their work on the doctoral student experience also highlight the role of socialisation in becoming a researcher. Within this they identify other students, professional communities, personal communities, and the university as all playing a role.

Take some time to visit https://ethos.bl.uk/Home.do, your own university library, or an appropriate place where theses are stored in your country or field of study.

Make a list of all the different kinds of people listed in the acknowledgements of three to five theses.

- What people stand out as being key to the success of other graduates?
- Which of these people are already in your networks?
- How could you develop your network to ensure you have the support you need?

These might be questions to also revisit at the end of this chapter.

Why is it important to develop a village?

Many of our greatest athletes have degrees in sports science. They know the exact formula for optimal training and yet they still surround themselves with support teams and experts. Similarly, many of the top businesspeople employ coaches and advisors. This is because sometimes knowing, doing, and being able to reflect at a distance are three very different things. There is the age-old saying that "a problem shared is a problem halved" but we might argue that sometimes you can't even see the problem when you are fixed in one place. Think of it this way: If you are climbing a mountain and it is shrouded in fog, you will never know how close you are to the top without some other sense of perspective. This, for us, is the beauty of building a village. You can have any number of different perspectives to draw upon. Research also shows that peer support is an important aspect of doctoral development and often enables researchers to have much more honest conversations than they feel able to have with supervisors (Wilson et al., 2022).

Furthermore, whilst this book goes some way to help you navigate the hidden curriculum of doctoral study, there is only so much we can fit into one book. More than this, subjects, institutions, and disciplines will have their own unique ways of working. Your village will be a valuable source for understanding this and perhaps for offering a sense of "belonging". You may also need multiple villages. For example, peers studying at your institution, but also more widely. For Jon, some of his best advice came from friends he made through the British Sociological Association postgraduate forum. These relationships go far beyond the end of the thesis and many of us continue to support each other years later.

As we highlighted in Chapter 3 through drawing upon McAlpine's (2012) notion of intertextual networking, your reading can also be a valuable way to build intellectual connections. It can also be a good basis for developing interpersonal connections. One thing that it took us both time to realise is that other academics love hearing from readers that have engaged with their work. Sometimes these conversations about a paper, concept, or idea can lead to lasting professional connections or even collaborations. In fact, we have both ended up co-authoring works with people as a result of doing this. However, it is important to highlight that we never set out with this in mind, but those shared interests can sometimes lead to other things.

Pay it forward

We are very much of the mindset that any relationship should have some form of reciprocity. There are a number of ways to achieve this. Yes, you may be a novice researcher, but we are all experts in something. Perhaps that might be in terms of professional or subject expertise. Or it might be more practical skills like how to navigate the jungle of admin systems, support with computer issues, or even just a friendly ear to listen when it is needed. What is important is that relationships within your networks should not be only one way.

However, this reciprocation may not always be simply between two people. After all, there is a stage where we may all need some support early on when we do not have the skills or the capacity to provide this for others. For a system to work where inexperienced researchers are supported, those who have built this experience are needed to help. This is where paying it forward comes into play. Even as a new doctoral researcher, you might have the skills and capacity to support someone thinking of applying to a doctoral programme. Equally, as you move through into later years you will have the insider knowledge to help those coming up behind you.

Activity: Thinking about connections

Make a list of what things people have helped you with recently related to your doctorate that you might be able to offer similar support for in future.

List three skills you have – these might be more general, for example:

- Are you a whizz with social media and good at connecting people?
- Are you a good listener and able to help people reflect on the challenges they face in life?
- Do you have professional networks that you can link other people into?
- Do you have experience of academia that you could share?
- Have you been at your institution a while and know how local systems operate such as room bookings or helpful professional services staff?

Now consider:

- How might you be able to share these skills with others?
- What practical actions could you take having completed this activity?

Critical friends

One of the most valuable relationships you can develop within your village is that of the critical friend. Costa and Kallick (1993) highlight that this is someone who can offer critique, be an advocate for your work, and ask provocative questions.

Good critical friends will:

- Offer supportive yet challenging advice.
- Help you gain a sense of perspective.
- Listen as much as they speak.
- Probably ask more questions that they will offer answers.

You might have more than one of these people in your network but their value is to be able to offer you a sounding board or a different perspective on the ideas you are immersed in. Sometimes we get so bogged down in our thoughts we often cannot see the wood for the trees. Likewise, the emotional nature of feedback also often benefits from someone with some distance from your work to help you find the gems of advice hidden within what often appears to be a pile of dirt.

Health and wellbeing support

The previous chapter looked at the notion of building balance in your personal-work-doctorate triangle (p. 9). Here, we also mentioned Petra Boynton's book *Being well in academia* (2021). Both of these can help you think about who you might need in your village to provide health and well-being support. From our experience, though, every doctoral researcher will experience highs and lows during the journey. For some these will be more extreme than others and in some cases your support village may really benefit from professionals as well as the more informal members we mention later in this chapter. Seeing others facing similar challenges can also help you make sense of your own experiences or be aware of how to navigate both the highs and lows of the doctorate. If you have health or disability-related needs, remember that the support services within and outside of the university are likely to be a key part of your support village. Talking to other students with similar needs can be helpful in identifying who might be useful to include in your village.

The doctorate is unlike other forms of studying you might have experienced. Whilst you are probably used to getting feedback, it is likely that it has been accompanied in the past by a grade. Having this objective sense of success can sometimes help anchor quite diverse feedback. In the case of doctoral writing though, comments such as "interesting" or "this needs more thought" can quite easily have multiple interpretations depending on our own frame of mind, which has the potential to amplify this sense of not being able to sense exactly how well you are doing. Furthermore, unlike taught courses, there is often also far more personal investment in the doctorate. This means that getting feedback can cause greater emotional stress and it is important to be aware of this and prepare your support networks early on.

Online versus offline

The reality of the part-time doctorate, though, is often one of isolation. Whilst you may (or may not) be in a cohort of other students, you are unlikely to be spending a lot of time in the same physical spaces. This is quite unlike the experiences of full-time doctoral students who are more likely to have shared office or social spaces where they might interact. This means some form of remote communication is likely to be important to maintain your connections to your peers.

These connections can be maintained privately either on a one-to-one or group basis, perhaps by e-mail, text message, or WhatsApp groups. Alternatively, they might take place in semi-public spaces, such as communities on a virtual learning environment (such as Moodle, Canvas, or Blackboard – if your institution provides it), or even in a more public space on a social media platform such as Twitter, Facebook, or LinkedIn. The way you might maintain your private or semi-public connections is likely to be determined by the tools and places you as individuals have access to or are encouraged to use by your institutions, so what we will focus upon in this chapter is how you might extend these into the more public spaces of social media.

The value of social media

The role of social media in the part-time doctorate is a recurring theme in this book. In fact, the authors of this book both connected through Twitter and their respective blogging academic projects. Using social media in specific ways can help you both explore and promote identities in ways that go beyond formal organisational structures. Whilst this book aims to be accessible and practical, for those of you interested in more theoretical discussions of this topic, Jon wrote two papers on how blogging and Twitter helped him reflect during the PhD (Rainford 2016a, 2016b). He is not the only one who has reflected on this, in fact across the wider literature others such as Bennett and Folley (2022) have highlighted the role social media can play in reducing feelings of isolation and confusion. Their own reflections as part-time doctoral researchers, combined with a small-scale qualitative project of 24 other doctoral researchers, offer interesting insights that resonated with Jon's experiences and some of those recounted to us. Whilst Wilson et al. (2022) also highlighted the value of peer-led support, this does not have to only come from within your institution. In fact, for many of you, you might find peers more aligned with your research who are based in other places.

We also include a caveat that the world of social media changes rapidly. A lot of this book is grounded in the past experiences of researchers, however the social media landscape changes regularly. It may be by the time you read this another platform is more prevalent than Twitter for academics. Doctoral researchers we have spoken to recently have mentioned Mastodon, Spoutible and Discord as becoming increasingly popular in the UK and US and Weibo in China. However, most of the principles in this chapter about connecting online can be translated to other platforms. We recommend you think about the value as opposed to the mechanics when reading on.

There are of course both pros and cons to using social media. Some of these more positive aspects outweigh the negatives, and what for us might be a positive might be a negative in your situation, so it is important to make your own assessments of what is right for you and your own needs. For example, there are some benefits that can be seen by others as a pitfall. Bennett and Folley (2022) argue that another pitfall of Twitter is its informal and simplistic nature. We would in some ways challenge this as a real benefit. It is through the ability to have more informal exchanges on Twitter that helped us realise that the academic space can be one of support regardless of your position within its more formal hierarchies. This informal nature can also help create deeper connections beyond more instrumental exchanges.

Some benefits

There are many benefits beyond the few listed here but some key ones for doctoral researchers are:

- **A network of support from people who "get it"** – The doctorate can be a strange and lonely journey and often some of the things that will consume your worries may only really be understood by those who have been there.
- **A space to test out emerging ideas** – Social media can be a good place to think through some of your ideas with others. Short form text in tweets or longer form in blog posts both can help you work through ideas before they are fully developed.
- **A hivemind of expertise** – This can often help alert you to new publications, conferences, or opportunities.
- **Accountability** – Sometimes working in isolation is hard. Being able to share your goals with others can help you create a sense of accountability. This can be formal, through activities such as #ShutUpAndWrite, or more informal by simply posting your goals online.
- **Getting to know people** – This goes beyond getting to know their work but also building connections with others. Often the people in your field will become colleagues or friends over time so developing these deeper connections can be valuable.
- **Being able to support others** – Building your village is about mutual benefits. Whilst you may not be able to give back to some more senior colleagues who have supported you, you can support those coming up behind you.

The pitfalls

There are some possible pitfalls you should be aware of.

- **Time vortex** – Social media can be a huge tool for procrastination. Whilst this can sometimes be useful, the time invested in social media might be better used on reading and writing.
- **Managing multiple identities** – Where you might be balancing an external persona in your field of work with a novice researcher identity, this can create tensions in what you feel you can and should post.
- **Ethics** – Can and should you share thoughts about your research, context, or participants? Public posts have a wide audience so you need to be sure you would be happy for people you are talking about to read them.
- **Permeance of digital communication** – Temporary thoughts can often become immortalised in a way that might not be desirable. Whilst yes, social media posts can be deleted, the digital footprint that might be left can have a greater permanence.
- **Confidence** – A certain level of confidence is needed to get the most out of social media, especially when you are unsure of your ideas. It may take time to build up from lurking and reading the ideas of others to posting your own content.
- **Emotionality** – Social media can be a harsh environment. Sometimes people post without thinking about the implications of their responses. This can negatively impact you if you are not prepared.
- **Professional expectations** – Does your use of social media conflict with professional standards or might you need to consider these in what or how you post?

How to make social media work for you?

There are as many ways to engage with social media as there are people using it. Some people are huge evangelists for social media, others are more sceptical. You can choose how and in what way you engage with its different formats. You will notice that this section has talked generally about social media and whilst there are books that deal in depth with different platforms such as Mark Carrigan's excellent *Social Media for Academics* (Carrigan, 2020a), the value of it in building your village is really beyond the specific functions of a single platform. However, you might want to pick one that works for you and start there. Carrigan has oscillated between evangelism and scepticism for Twitter over the years. In fact, he was the one who introduced Jon to the value of the platform at the British Sociological Association conference back in 2012. In his book he offers more comprehensive guidance on how to make social media work for you.

The forms of social media that are most likely to work for you are ones that focus on written text. This can be short form, such as on Twitter; longer form on blogging platforms (such as Medium, WordPress, or Substack); or a mixture of the two as you might find on LinkedIn. For Jon and Kay, Twitter has been the platform of choice, although LinkedIn and Mastodon have become an increasing part of Jon's networking over the past year. Whilst there are downsides to using social media, both authors of this book are huge proponents of its value. Having met through Twitter and managed a lot of this book through it, we see it as integral to our academic lives and as a way of connecting with many colleagues. Carrigan (2020b) has framed Twitter as having "valuable pockets of interaction" in a recent blog post, which is a really useful way of thinking about it. There is no doubt that Twitter can be polarising and harbour negativity, but for us it's outweighed by the value it can add.

Following specific hashtags on social media can be a useful way to find these pockets of interaction and to build your village. You will find hashtags associated with many academic conferences. These can be a good way to interact with people in your field or to start conversations you might want to continue offline. Beyond conferences, hashtags can also work as a filtering mechanism for general posts such as #PhDChat or #ThrivingPartTime that are not time specific. Other hashtags can be used in a more time-limited way and be associated with synchronous Twitter chats such as #VirtualNotViral, #LTHEChat, or #CRMethodsChat.

We both have limits though, taking regular social media breaks where needed, choosing not to engage (and to use the block/filter options where necessary), and thinking about who our audiences are and why we post certain content. You might also decide to create a separate social media account for your research and to only have this on some devices. This can be a sensible way to engage in a manageable way that supports as opposed to hinders your research.

Confidence and feeling like an imposter

In some ways, this speaks to the issues we discussed in Chapter 3 on identity. Imposter syndrome is a real thing. Having expertise outside of academia often falls out of our memory and we can feel like the new kid on the playground again. This is even more evident when social media often feels like a place where people talk a lot about the good things that are happening to them or promote all the amazing work they (appear to be) doing. However, it is important to remember that social media is where people put their highlight reels on display. Try not to compare your normal days to their best days and remember that whilst you might be new to a field, you have lots of enthusiasm, experience, and ideas to bring to conversations, some of which those who have been around for a while may really value.

When you start interacting with people who are more experienced in a field, it can also feel daunting to strike up a conversation. One of our top tips is to try and find organic points of entry. Maybe you have liked something they have written, or perhaps agree with something they have said. This can be a good way into replying to them and gradually building links. You might also want to focus on non-academic topics initially. Pets are a perennial favourite – see the #AcademicsWithCats or #AcademicsWithDogs hashtags for inspiration. This is not to say you should only talk about pets, but in forming bonds with people on a human level, it can make those more academic discussions seem less daunting.

Building your academic village

You will have realised that many of the people you need in your village can be specific to your doctoral journey. The connections and bonds formed during the doctorate do not have to end when you submit that thesis. In fact, ensuring you have a network to sustain you for the next steps is important. Whether or not you are planning a career in academia, you are probably going to want to stay connected to your subject area in some way. Hopefully you will want to share the findings of your years of research and maybe even continue to develop it. To do so, you may need to find some new critical friends or collaborators. As a part-time doctoral researcher, it can be harder to develop these connections, so in this section we will highlight some potential ways to do this.

It is worth taking a moment to consider where you might find people with shared interests in academia. Similarly, you might consider what areas you have interesting ideas to contribute to. The obvious one might be the subject, topic, or discipline you are researching, but this should not limit you. It might be that you are using the work of a particular theorist around whom there are interested groups focusing upon their work. Alternatively, it may be that you are using a method or approach in your empirical work that could create some connections beyond the specific subject or discipline within which you might have previously identified. Building wider connections can allow you to enrich your own villages, which can be transformative.

Subject associations

What is available to you is likely to vary based upon the discipline your research aligns and your own geographical location. Trying to document these could be a book in and of itself. To find out about relevant associations and possible postgraduate groups, ask your supervisor and peers who the most useful subject associations are that align with your research. Most subject associations will have postgraduate membership rates (although be prepared that sometimes you may have to make the case that as a part-time researcher you are entitled to this – you are, fight for it).

Many associations will also have dedicated postgraduate groups or special events. These can be a great place to build connections with other researchers outside of your institution. If you decide to follow an academic career, many of these other researchers are also likely to be future colleagues or collaborators. Even more importantly, these are people on a similar journey who can provide mutual support and who may be able to offer advice and guidance, as hopefully you will to those who are following on the journey behind you.

Conferences

Conferences and seminars come in all shapes and sizes, from huge international conferences with several thousand delegates in big convention centres all the way down to intimate groups of less than ten people. However, even within the largest conferences there are likely to be smaller streams (collections of sessions linked by a topic or theme) or sessions (individual groups of presentations, workshops, or papers). Within these, group sizes can often be smaller. This means that even at the largest of conferences, you may find you bump into the same people regularly. It is likely that these people might belong in your village. Burford and Henderson (2023), *Making sense of academic conferences: presenting, participating and organising*, will help demystify a lot of what conferences are for – and should you wish to, how to organise your own.

Academia in general is built on networks and relationships. Sometimes, as an outsider these can look and feel cliquey. This is not always intentional; it is just that some people will only see each other at such events. In this situation, don't be afraid to introduce yourself to people. A great way to do this is to make contact to follow up after you have heard them speak about their research. Find something you found interesting or want to know more about;

this can often be a good basis for finding out more about the field and their work. You may even find they introduce you to others (although do not take offence if they don't).

Especially as a part-time researcher, you might have limited time and resources to participate in all the conferences you might want to, so think about what matters most to you at this stage in your journey. If it is meeting fellow doctoral researchers, then look for conferences and workshops focused on postgraduate issues. If you are looking to expand your wider networks, try to find ones aligned with your field of research. Of course, one of the biggest challenges can be not knowing where you fit. This sometimes means trial and error is required – it is OK to realise that maybe on reflection people don't belong in your village.

Real-world reflection – exploring other villages

We asked a number of current and recent doctoral researchers who was in their village. As you can imagine, the list was very varied, but we thought we would share some of them and their reasons why:

- **Their doctoral cohort**: People going through the same degree in the same institution. Valuable as they often are tackling the same issues.
- **Women in Academia support network**: Issue-based networks can be useful for thinking about specific challenges.
- **National subject networks**: These varied based on researchers' focuses but often were essential for helping them get to know the field and current issues related to their research field.

- **Twitter**: This was often seen as a major lifeline for finding support, sharing experiences, and feeling part of a community.
- **Self-support groups**: Many researchers talked about having to build their own groups as they could not find existing ones that met their needs. These were both institutional and more far reaching in some cases, with varying degrees of formality.

Moving villages

However beneficial others can be on your academic journey, sometimes it is important to know when to disconnect with people. It may be that these relationships that were once valuable stop being mutually beneficial. It may be that something that once felt useful becomes a burden, or a drain on your time. This is OK to acknowledge and do something about (in fact, being able to see this can be very healthy). What is important is that you try to end connections amicably as you never know when your paths might cross again.

Activity: How can I apply this to my own doctorate?

Draw a table with three columns: "connections you have," "connections that would be helpful," and "connections that you need to develop."

Under each of these columns, think through all the people that might be involved in your journey:

- Start with those you have identified in the activities in this chapter.

- Revisit your notes from Chapters 2, 3, and 6 and see if there are any more to add.

Using this list, consider:

- Are these connections mutually beneficial or just serving your needs?
- How could you balance this out by making connections to support others?

Remember that building a village is about creating mutual benefit with your networks.

What you have discovered in this chapter would make a useful addition to your "route map" created in Chapter 2. We suggest that you revisit your map and continue to annotate it, based on your learning in each subsequent chapter.

Researchers recommend ...

- Get involved with a range of networks both inside and outside of your institution, but put your energy into the ones that are aligned with your own needs.
- Relationships are reciprocal. Whilst you may not be able to pay back what others give you, take the chance to pay it forward and support others on their journey.
- Finding others who "get it" to talk to when it all gets too challenging can be invaluable for your well-being.
- Sometimes finding your village is actually about building your village!

Where can I find out more?

Rui He's (2021) blog on the "loop-building" initiative also helps apply some of these ideas to their own doctorate.

If you are interested in the use of conferences to build your village, James Burford and Emily Henderson's (2023) *Making Sense of Academic Conferences: Presenting, Participating and Organising*, also in the Insiders Guide series, is likely to be a valuable starting point.

Note

1 Previously the authors have talked about building a tribe, and this metaphor is used in the linked blog post. We have decided to shift the metaphor to that of a village to acknowledge the problematic nature of appropriating terminology from indigenous cultures.

References

Bennett, L. and Folley, S. (2022) 'Doctoral candidates' experiences of social media: I don't think I could do the PhD without it', in Sheldon, J. and Sheppard, V. (eds.) *Online Communities for doctoral researchers and their supervisors*. Abingdon: Routledge.

Boynton, P. (2021) *Being Well in Academia*, Abingdon: Routledge.

Burford, J. and Henderson, E.F. (2023) *Making Sense of Academic Conferences: Presenting, Participating and Organising*, Abingdon: Routledge.

Carrigan, M. (2020a) *Social Media for Academics* (2nd edition), London: Sage.

Carrigan, M. (2020b) 'Twitter hybridises the personal and the professional in the most subtly violent manner'. https://postpandemicuniversity. net/2020/12/04/twitter-hybridises-the-personal-and-the-professional-in-the-most-subtly-violent-manner-leading-work-to-become-life-and-life-to-become-work/

Costa, A. L., & Kallick, B. (1993) 'Through the Lens of a Critical Friend', *Educational Leadership*, 51, 49–49. Available at: https://educandojuntos.cl/wp-content/uploads/2017/12/through_the_lens_of_a_critical_friend.pdf (Accessed 11 April 2022).

Elliot, D. L., Bengtsen, S. S. E., Guccione, K. and Kobayashi, S. (2020) *The Hidden Curriculum in Doctoral Education*. Basingstoke: Palgrave Macmillan.

Gardner, S. K. and Gopaul, B. (2012) 'The part-time doctoral student experience', *International Journal of Doctoral Studies*, 7, 63–78. doi:10.28945/1561

He, R. (2021) "The 'loop-building' initiative', *The hidden curriculum in doctoral education*'. Available at: https://drhiddencurriculum.wordpress.com/2021/08/09/the-loop-building-initiative/ (Accessed 26 July 2022).

McAlpine, L. (2012) 'Identity-trajectories: Doctoral journeys from past to present to future', *The Australian Universities' Review*, 54(1), 38–46. https://search.informit.org/doi/10.3316/ielapa.424355529639257

Rainford, J. (2016a) 'Becoming a doctoral researcher in a digital world: Reflections on the role of Twitter for reflexivity and the internal conversation', *E-Learning and Digital Media*, 13(1–2), 99–105. doi:10.1177/2042753016672380

Rainford, J. (2016b) 'Making internal conversations public: Reflexivity of the connected doctoral researcher and its transmission beyond the walls of the academy', *Journal of Applied Social Theory*, 1(1), 44–60. Available at: http://socialtheoryapplied.com/journal/jast/article/view/14

Wilson C, Arshad R, Sapouna M, et al. (2022) 'PGR Connections': Using an online peer- learning pedagogy to support doctoral researchers, *Innovations in Education and Teaching International*, 1–11 doi: 10.1080/14703297.2022.2141292

8 Moving on from this book

By the end of this chapter you will

- Consider what you are looking to achieve over the next year, and the small steps that will get you there.
- Return to thinking about the bigger picture of your doctoral work, in the context of your future research career.
- Have planned for the end, and considered how to know when you have "finished" your doctorate.

What's in store

Now you have made it to through the majority of this book, this chapter will help you pull all those thoughts, ideas, and plans together. Hopefully you have worked through lots of the activities and have some clear actions, but this chapter might help you connect the dots into an actionable plan. You might want to even work through this chapter more than once at different stages. Moving on might mean taking practical action after your first read, early in your doctorate. Moving on could also be focused on what's next after you submit. Either way, we hope this chapter will offer some clarity on what's next.

DOI : 10.4324/9781003223931-9

Looking beyond this book

In the final chapter of this book we want to enable you to bring together all your learning you have taken away from the chapters that preceded it. We want to close down our handbook by doing two things. Firstly by helping you to keep up momentum for the kinds of reflective mapping and planning activities you have completed, so that you can sustain the active practice of navigating your doctorate and charting your own pathway through it. Secondly, we want to look ahead at what is likely to be on the horizon for you as you progress and move towards completion of your doctorate, and signpost you to some follow-on resources that you can work with when the time is right for you.

If you have skimmed through this book to get a feel for the landscape and key messages about doing a part-time doctorate, or dipped in and out of the various chapters and taken in some of the ideas and put them into practice, we consider that a successful outcome, and thank you for spending time with our words. We know that others among our readers will have been moving through the book in a more linear methodical way, completing each reflective activity before moving to the next, and we also thank you for engaging with the facilitative exercises we have developed for you. Others still will have selected certain chapters to prioritise, perhaps looking for enlightenment on a particular issue, or to troubleshoot a perceived problem. As we talked about at length in Chapter 2, there is no right way to do a part-time doctorate, and navigating the process to extract what you personally need, at the right time for you, is an essential skill of doctoral researchers. Your engagement with this book is no different – please take what you need. However, as you have landed here at this final chapter, we invite you to take a pause to consider how the ideas you have encountered in this book have validated what you already know about the challenges and opportunities of a part-time doctorate, and how the book has challenged your thinking or inspired you to make a change in your approach. Our primary aim as authors, and the reason we felt most compelled to write this volume, is to provide insights that are of practical use to you. We hope that whatever stage you are at in your doctorate, this has been the case. We also hope that this book has been useful to you in remembering why you are here today, doing your part-time doctorate, and in recognising the professional and personal value it is bringing to you. The following activity makes use of Bryan and Guccione's (2018) four domains of doctoral value model and will help you to recognise the value you are receiving from your studies.

Activity: Charting the value of your doctorate

Use the following boxes to note how you perceive the value of your doctorate in each of the four domains. Think about the value added by both formal development opportunities and the informal learning spaces or chance encounters you have had with others. Are there any areas in which you want to seek to draw down additional value as you move forward? Try to be as honest as you can, remembering that the outcomes of this activity are just for you.

Use the final box to note if and how the different factors influence your sense of value added, positively or negatively.

Skills and competencies: What are your developing areas of expertise? Think about your research skills and also universally applicable skills such as communication, decision-making, and project management.	Career development opportunities: What new experiences or responsibilities have you engaged with or taken on? What opportunities are you now eligible for?
People, communities, and networks: Who have you had the opportunity to engage with and learn from? Who have you taught, influenced, or led?	Personal growth and world view: How has your view of yourself and of the world changed? How do you now see yourself in relation to others?

How does each of the factors below influence how I perceive the value of my doctorate?
The way my course is set up and the networks and resources offered to me:
The stage I am at in my doctorate:
My relationship with my supervisors(s):
The attitudes of my current or future employers:
The opinions of my family or social groups:
Other:

We encourage you to keep returning to the lists you have created as you progress through the course of your doctorate, adding to them as you go and charting the value your studies are bringing to you. Firstly, this awareness may be useful to you as a way of recognising your professional and personal growth, highlighting any gaps in this you might want to fill, and helping you to consider how you might articulate this to your current or future employers. Secondly, this activity will be a useful source of encouragement in tougher times as you navigate the more challenging parts of your doctorate, acting as a way of reminding yourself that it is worth persevering to the finish line.

How to move towards an exit plan

We intended that this book would provide you with guidance to help you to marshal your thoughts into a plan that works for you. Chapter 2 introduced you to the idea of there being no one right way to move through your doctorate and no single "correct" end point or destination. In supporting you to move on from these initial reflections, we suggest that you begin to consider the doctoral "finish line." Whatever point you are at in your doctorate it is always worth considering how your plans and the actions that come out of them are leading you to the end point. Whilst this might feel a bit premature, especially if you are in the early stages of your doctorate, having a sense of what is required from you to complete your doctorate brings greater awareness of what you will submit for examination, and allows you to anticipate what will be required of you rather than be taken by surprise. This reduces the sense of heading into the unknown, which is likely to make you feel apprehensive or overwhelmed and lead you into periods of procrastination. Having a plan creates a feeling of control. It breaks down a large task into more manageable pieces that can be completed and ticked off and allows you to work backwards to make sure that you meet your deadline, tracking your progress as you go, which is good for morale in the final phases. Some simple actions you can take as soon as possible are to look at some successfully defended doctoral theses from your degree type, discipline, and institution – see what you are aiming to produce; talk to part-time researchers who have just completed their doctorate – what are their words of advice?; and create an exit plan. You will find a guide to this as follows:

1. Find out your final thesis submission deadline from your department or university research office and note it in your diary.
2. Consider if you personally want to set a deadline sooner than your final cutoff date. This may be influenced by your employer, your financial circumstances, or a life event. Make sure you discuss and communicate your deadline with your supervisors and anyone else who can help you to succeed with your goal. Add this date to your diary.
3. Working backwards from your thesis submission date, calculate how much time you have from now until then. Depending on where you are in the doctoral process, this may be more appropriate for you to do in months, weeks, or days. Note the number you calculate.
4. Adjust that number to account for working at a sustainable pace. Make sure you allocate yourself regular time off to rest and recharge so that you don't burn out. Take out any days you do paid work and any days you volunteer, work in the home, or have caring responsibilities. Take out festival holidays you will want to enjoy, family birthdays, or planned trips. This is really worth doing. Making a plan you cannot stick with will create stress and reduce your motivation.
5. Note your new number (or months, weeks, days) and make a template timeline however you prefer, using a notebook and pen or your favourite productivity or project management software (we covered some of these in Chapter 5). Block out all your working days, family or caring days, rest days, and holidays (as above). Allocate the final couple of weeks solely for thesis formatting, printing, technical issues, and final checks, as experience tells us you will need this.

6. Now populate your timeline with an outline of your plan. Your plan will be unique to you, and tailored to your degree type and project. As well as you can, factor in time for drafting and redrafting of written materials, time waiting for feedback from your supervisors, and time waiting for any permissions or resources that you will need. Look at the riskier elements (novel experiments, recruiting participants, or awaiting editorial permissions, for example) and factor in more time for these. Note that there probably isn't enough time to do one thing at a time and factor in the parallel processes of reading and writing, of researching and writing, and of career development and project work.
7. Share this with your supervisors and anyone else who needs to know.

To keep you on track with your plan, we recommend that you revisit any activities you have begun throughout this book (for the full list see the Activity Map on p. 9) and continue to use them to regularly reflect on and audit your doctoral experience. Taking time out to stop and consider how things are going, who can help you, and how you are working with others around you will help you to sustain a sense of progress and control, and that elusive feeling of being "on track." Additionally, regularly checking in with yourself will help you to maintain progress on your doctorate and, in parallel, to plan your ongoing professional and career development in the mid and long term. This will support you to make sure that the actions you take in the coming months will lead you towards the end-point goals you are aiming to achieve, by your deadline, and importantly, at a pace you can sustain. Why not make a note in your diary to revisit the thinking and planning you have already done as prompted by this book? Perhaps take yourself out for a coffee or lunch in two or three months' time and review how things are going. Ask yourself, did you have the conversations you needed to have? Did you stick to the plans you made for yourself? There are likely to be other review points that occur as part of your doctorate too, such as annual progress reviews with your supervisory team, and other formal landmarks of degree progression involving documents or meetings to be completed. If you are working alongside your doctorate, you may be reviewing things with your employer too. Keeping your reflective planning documents "live" and up to date will support these reflective reviews too, and you can of course choose the ideas and messages you are comfortable with sharing, as appropriate.

Troubleshooting a loss of motivation

We wanted to return to the idea of sustaining motivation and momentum, as we feel that challenges to momentum are a certain feature of all types of part-time doctorate. Losing motivation from time to time is almost universal to every doctoral researcher we have known, ourselves included. The following helpful list of ideas for regaining your motivational mojo have been generated by your doctoral peers through the part-time doctorate workshops and open tweet chats we have hosted in recent years. They resonate well with our own experience of supervising and developing a vast variety of doctoral researchers from across a wide range of degree types and disciplines. We hope you might see yourself reflected here too, and find some of these ideas useful when you are feeling low in inspiration.

Remind yourself that feeling under-motivated sometimes is quite normal. Practice being OK with that and know that it is not a reflection of your intelligence or your ability.

Notice what causes you to lose momentum. Is it long pauses in your study? Starting something new? Finishing something off? Supervisory feedback? Spending time in your own head? Overworking? Or something else? Knowing the cause can help you figure out what to do about it, and who to talk to about it.

Don't compare your insides with others' outsides. You may look around you and see everyone doing well, but inside they will be experiencing self-doubts too.

Remember that avoiding your doctoral work never leads to a positive outcome. You can use as much energy on avoidance tactics that also leave you feeling guilty or disheartened. As time ticks by, avoiding your work creates stress for you and those around you.

Overcome your "unknowns." Of course we tend to prefer doing things we know how to do. If you don't know how to approach something, go and find out. Define the task. Use your supervisors, your doctoral peers, your networks, and online communities. Ask a question, get an answer.

Take a break. Balancing working time with breaks from working or a change of task helps you to focus on the task at hand. If you need a break of minutes, days, or weeks, then acknowledge that formally, communicate with your supervisors, and take time off to restore your energy levels.

Look at your current plan. Is it unrealistic, leaving you always behind schedule and frustrated? Make a new plan, one that is realistic and you can stick to.

Set time limits. Rather than seeing doctoral work as a never-ending commitment that requires long days to get anything meaningful done, set aside short slots of time to do focused work. You won't "find time" so *make* time and preserve it in your diary. You are worth your own attention.

Aim to do just one thing in any given working slot. Set yourself a goal that you can achieve in the time you have, for example, "read one article" or "write five sentences about topic X." Choose the most difficult task and do it first, when you have the most energy.

Once you have got yourself started, stay started by not working to exhaustion. Putting down your day's work once your task or time limit is completed, and while you are still enjoying it, means that you will be keen to come back to it at the next allocated session.

Track and note your progress. On long projects it can be difficult to see how far you have come, when there is still so much to do. Make sure you are noting what you have achieved as well as what you still need to do. Celebrate the small milestones as well as the big ones.

If you are stuck, let people know you are stuck. That may be a supervisor, colleague, mentor, co-researcher, friend, or family member. Find a person who will listen to you talk about your research and what you are stuck with. Talk it through, and see what ideas come to mind. Write them down and take it from there.

In some cases, changing supervisor, degree type, or institution may be the answer for you. This is not always possible, and making a substantial change requires you to consult the right people at your university and a potential new university. But, if you have invested significant time in trying to make your doctorate work and are not receiving the support or resources you need, consider how you can make that change.

How to recognise when you have finished your doctorate

A topic we discuss over and over again with the doctoral researchers we meet is how to recognise when the end is really the end, and the thesis is "finished." Given our

prior advice concerning setting an end date and working backwards, this might seem a strange point to make.
Yet, despite regular reflection, forward "exit planning,"
and the setting of hard deadlines, we hear from researchers that the end felt rushed, or that the thesis didn't feel
complete, or that they keep rewriting their argument to
take in new literature. This feeling is very common indeed
and what we are actually hearing here is that researchers
are experiencing a sense of ambiguity about what constitutes "enough" for a doctoral thesis, and what standard of
writing is "good enough" to be judged favourably. As you
move towards the end, it will benefit you to keep certain
ideas in mind:

You are submitting a "work in progress." Your doctoral thesis represents a status update, or a "snapshot" in time. It communicates what you have
achieved with your research in the time you have
available. It documents your unique contribution
to what is known on this topic. You do not have to
"complete" the research, or answer all the possible
further questions it generated. Are the gaps you feel
inclined to fill actually real holes in your argument
that render it unconvincing? Or are they additional
work that follows up new lines of investigation? Your
examiners expect there to be "limitations to the
study" and "further work arising," and these are very
likely to be explicit sections within your thesis which
you can use to explain how you prioritise your work,
and what you would like to do next.

**Many researchers adjust their expectations during
the course of their doctorate**. As you progress
in your field and your knowledge grows as well as
does the existing literature base, you will evaluate

ideas differently and naturally change your priorities based on your developing expertise. What once seemed of key importance may later fall away as you define your niche. Additionally, as you become familiar with the practicalities of doing research and the time it takes to do it well, you will want to pare back the ambitious plans you laid out at a time when you didn't have such knowledge. Reducing scope and focusing on a coherent argument is to your benefit.

Feeling insecure about the value of your contribution is normal. Remember that you are the expert in your field, and so you are highly familiar and closely involved in what you are researching. By the end of your doctorate, the immersion in the topic that goes hand in hand with growing expertise can mean that your research no longer surprises you, or feels exciting or novel any more. Losing confidence in the originality or in the meaningfulness of your doctoral work is part of the motivational rollercoaster we ride. Remember that your opinion is skewed and you can't objectively evaluate your work. Talk to others who are energised by it, and in turn hear about their work.

New literature will always keep being published! It can feel that each time you integrate a new article into your literature review or discussion, another two interesting articles appear and get on the "to read" list. Of course, new papers are published continuously and you want to be thorough. However, repeated last minute searching and checking for new literature is a pitfall to avoid in the later stages. Don't be tempted to keep monitoring all channels for new outputs in order to add it; this will cycle and delay you. Additionally, whilst it is a very frustrating situation to have your exact topic or research question published by another researcher at a stage when you cannot change focus, this doesn't mean that you have to exclude it from your thesis.

The doctorate is a pass or fail qualification. Contrary to previous qualifications you hold, there is no top grade or highest score that is available to you. A completed thesis that offers a cogent argument, defines what you have done, states clearly how and why you did it, and documents that you yourself completed the body of work described, is what is needed. Think about what is required for a doctoral thesis, and then fulfil those requirements. Good enough is good enough. You can put further time into any published work that comes from your thesis, which will have far greater reach, readership, and impact.

A finished thesis is better than a perfect thesis! Aiming for perfection can waste your time and energy, as it is an unattainable goal. However long you spend checking, refining, proofreading, polishing, and rechecking, you will always find some small mistakes (or some missing new literature) after you have submitted it. Not to worry! You can be listing or even doing these self-identified "corrections" whilst you await your examiner's feedback, or viva examination.

Making sure your thesis is submitted on time is your responsibility, and you are the person who must make the decision on when to stop. Do consider the advice forthcoming from your supervisors and balance this with your needs, and do compare your work to other successfully examined theses, but remember that the final decision is yours to make.

Activity: Your "real-world reflection" – a letter to your future self

Throughout this book you will have become used to seeing our regular real-world reflections. These are narratives shared with us by part-time researchers in the course of our research. In this final chapter we want to invite you to write your own narrative. We suggest that this takes the form of a "letter to your future self." This is a writing device that you can use to articulate your thoughts and feelings here and now, and that you can also use to reset, inspire, motivate, comfort, or amuse yourself at a future point.

This letter is just for you, and you can choose what it should contain, when it should be opened, and how to write it. Write kindly, in the tone and style you most enjoy reading. This could be a physical paper letter on your finest stationery that you have a friend or colleague put into the post. It could be a document attached to a meeting with yourself in your e-Calendar or it might be a file you pop into your "Doctoral Thesis" folder to find when you most need it.

We suggest you might want to tell your future self some of the following:

- What you are working on and why.
- How it's going for you.
- Something you've just learned that resonated with you.
- Your relationships to the people who are supporting you.
- How far you have come since starting your doctorate.
- The things that are important to you right now.
- Your biggest unknowns or uncertainties.

- What you are enjoying, and not enjoying.
- How you are feeling about the future.
- Your career or personal ambitions for after the doctorate.
- New things you want to do or learn soon.
- Any changes to your professional life or approach you want to make.
- And anything else that you like too – a joke, a meme, a picture.

Contribute to the Thriving Part-Time community

One final note of invitation. If you have been motivated by this book, if you had a moment of insight or realisation, if you engaged with the activities we designed for you, or if you have additional ideas and tips that we have not included here, please let us know on social media using the hashtag #ThrivingPartTime – we love to see how you approach the mapping activities and appreciate your creative approaches to planning your part-time doctorate.

If you have a different or unique experience of doing a part-time doctorate that we have not discussed, we would love for you to write a blog post for our Thriving Part-Time community. The Thriving Part-Time blog that accompanies this book houses a collection of posts by a range of authors. The narratives we publish come exclusively from those who have completed or are undertaking part-time doctorates. Its content is therefore only as rich as the range of contributions that are made. If you do not see yourself or people like you represented in this book, we would particularly love to include your story, and learn from your experiences. Anonymous contributions are welcomed.

Researchers recommend ...

- Keeping things in perspective by regularly checking back in on your plans. There will be highs and lows as you progress through your doctorate, but you have all the tools you need to sustain momentum and to manage the more challenging times.
- Understanding that planning for the end is important and that your doctoral project is not something you will ever "finish." Your thesis, at the point of submission, is a snapshot in time that presents a coherent contribution to the field.
- That you revisit the activities you have begun in the book and continue to plan for your future development, both in the mid and long term, making sure the actions you take in the immediate weeks will lead you towards your larger goals.

Where can I find out more?

Completing Your EdD: The Essential Guide to the Doctor of Education, by Iona Burnell Reilly and Jodi Roffey-Barentsen (2020), provides a thorough and comprehensive guide intended to accompany you as you successfully progress through your EdD.

Doctoral Research by Distance is a multi-level resource bank and support community for anyone doing their doctorate as a distance learner. The team behind this research-informed project aim to share practical examples, stories, and strategies. https://doctoralresearchbydistance. wordpress.com/ There is also a related book (forthcoming) in the Insiders Guide series by Katrina McChesney,

James Burford, Liezel Frick, and Tseen Khoo entitled *Doing Doctoral Research by Distance: Navigating Off-campus, Online, Hybrid, and Cross-national Doctoral Study*.

If you are completing a thesis by publication, we recommend Shannon Mason and Margaret Merga's (2022) online resource-bank which contains FAQs, stories from researchers, and even a bank of real successfully defended theses containing published works that you can download and read. https://thesisbypublication.com/. There is also a book in the insider series by Lynn P. Nygaard and Kristin Solli (2020), *Strategies for Writing a Thesis by Publication in the Social Sciences and Humanities*, which is likely to be valuable to those of you on this path.

Dr Holly Prescott's blog – *PostGradual: The PhD Careers Blog* – is a resource for all researchers considering options for your next role. It is relevant to all types of doctorate, and takes a UK focus: https://phd-careers.co.uk/about/. In addition, many universities' careers services are open to doctoral researchers and increasingly commonly run specific workshops, 1:1 consultations, and employer networking events for doctoral graduates.

The book *Publishing from your Doctoral Research* by Janet Salmons and Helen Kara (2020) takes a detailed look at different strategies for publishing your findings and presents them in a practical and accessible way. This is also a great place to map out what's next so that your research can have the greatest impact possible.

References

Bryan, B. and Guccione, K. (2018) 'Was it worth it? A qualitative exploration of graduate perceptions of doctoral value'. *Higher Education Research and Development*, 37(6), 1124–1140. doi: 10.1080/07294360.2018.1479378

Burnell, I. and Roffey-Barentsen, J. (2020) *Completing Your EdD: The Essential Guide to the Doctor of Education*. Bingley: Emerald Group Publishing Limited.

Mason, S. and Merga, M. (2022) *Thesis by publication*. Available at: https://thesisbypublication.com/ (Accessed 2 November 2022).

McChesney, K., Burford, J., Frick, L. and Khoo, T. (forthcoming) *Doing Doctoral Research by Distance: Navigating Off-campus, Online, Hybrid, and Cross-national Doctoral Study*. Abingdon: Routledge.

Nygaard, L.P. and Solli, K. (2020) *Strategies for Writing a Thesis by Publication in the Social sciences and Humanities*. Abingdon: Routledge.

Prescott, H. (2022) *PostGradual: The PhD Careers Blog*. Available at: https://phd-careers.co.uk/blog/ (Accessed 2 November 2022).

Salmons, J. and Kara, H. (2020) *Publishing from your Doctoral Research. Create and Use a Publication Strategy*. Abingdon: Routledge.

Index

Taylor & Francis Group
an **informa** business

Taylor & Francis eBooks

www.taylorfrancis.com

A single destination for eBooks from Taylor & Francis
with increased functionality and an improved user
experience to meet the needs of our customers.

90,000+ eBooks of award-winning academic content in
Humanities, Social Science, Science, Technology, Engineering,
and Medical written by a global network of editors and authors.

TAYLOR & FRANCIS EBOOKS OFFERS:

A streamlined
experience for
our library
customers

A single point
of discovery
for all of our
eBook content

Improved
search and
discovery of
content at both
book and
chapter level

REQUEST A FREE TRIAL
support@taylorfrancis.com

For Product Safety Concerns and Information please contact our EU representative GPSR@taylorandfrancis.com Taylor & Francis Verlag GmbH, Kaufingerstraße 24, 80331 München, Germany

Batch number: 08153762

Printed by Printforce, the Netherlands